DELHI

AND ITS NEIGHBOURHOOD

BY

Y. D. SHARMA

M. A., D. Phil. (Oxon.)

PUBLISHED BY THE DIRECTOR GENERAL
ARCHAEOLOGICAL SURVEY OF INDIA
NEW DELHI
2001

First edition, 1964
Second edition, 1974
Reprinted, 1982
Reprinted, 1990
Reprinted, 2001

Price : Rs. 50.00

PRINTED AT BENGAL OFFSET WORKS, NEW DELHI

CONTENTS

PAGE

PAGE

PREFACE

Since the appearance of the first edition of this book in 1964, new discoveries have been made in Delhi. The most illuminating among these is the find of a rock-edict of Aśoka. Less sensational, but no less elucidating for Delhi's past, are the results of the recent excavations at Purana-Qila. The present edition, which has been fully revised, includes brief details of all these discoveries, Some new illustrations have also been added in this edition. The addition of the index to monuments, it is hoped, will enhance its utility.

The transliteration of Persian words and names poses certain difficulties in a book of this nature which is intended primarily for the lay visitor but provides also information for a leisurely and more inquisitive itinerant. A *via media* has, therefore, been struck. The names of localities and popular monuments have been spelt as shown in the *Delhi Guide Map* published by the Survey of India with minor modifications, and without any diacritical marks. Where the name of such a monument occurs for the first time, its proper spelling is given in brackets. Otherwise the Arabic letters have been transliterated in accordance with the principles usually followed in the *Epigraphia Indica-Arabic and Persian Supplement* published by the Archaeological Survey of India. Letter *zāl* has, however, been represented by dh, *swād* by ṣ and *zwad* by ẓ. Words like sultan, sarai etc., which have become part of English language, have been printed without diacritical marks. The transliteration of words of Sanskrit Hindi or indigenous origin follows the principles for these languages.

I am grateful to my colleagues Dr Z. A. Desai, Shri M. C. Joshi and Shri W.H. Siddiqi for their several suggestions which have been incorporated in this edition. I must also acknowledge with thanks the assistance of several other colleagues: Shri Narendra Nath has gone through the proofs and has checked the transliterated spelling, Shri S. N. Jaiswal has prepared the index to monuments, Shri B. P. Asthana has taken some new photographs specially for this edition, Shri S. S. Saar has prepared the map of Delhi and the cover of this edition and Shri M. S. Mani the two plans.

New Delhi Y. D. SHARMA
7th January 1974

DELHI AND ITS NEIGHBOURHOOD

1. INTRODUCTION

FEW CITIES IN INDIA COULD CLAIM THE LONG CONTINUITY and status that Delhi has enjoyed. In the dim proto-historic past, at the site of the sixteenth century citadel Purana-Qila (Qal'a-i-Kuhna) lay perhaps Indra prastha, capital of the heroes of the epic *Mahābhārata*. This settlement, known by different names at different times, has been recently excavated by the Archaeological Survey of India on a large scale revealing a continuous occupation from the Mauryan to Early Mughal period —from the third century B.C. to the sixteenth century A.D. Earlier relics of the *Mahābhārata* age, if represented by the characteristic Painted Grey Ware, as believed by some scholars, have turned up among the rubbish and débris of later dates, evading, thus, the archaeologist's anticipated horizons, yet prompting him not to relinquish the search for a distinct settlement of the Painted Grey Ware people in Delhi.

A glorious chapter to Delhi's history was added as recently as 1966 with the discovery of an inscription of the Maurya emperor Aśoka (273-36 B.C.) engraved on a rugged rock of an outcrop of the Aravallis, near Srinivas-puri, west of Kalkaji temple (pp. 10, 105).

In the eighth century, or a little earlier, a large temple existed at the site of the Sultan Ghārī's tomb, 8 km west of the Qutb-Minar. The temple was erected probably by some feudatory of the Pratīhāras. In any case, the Tomar Rajputs established themselves in the hills south of Delhi, in the ninth or tenth century. Later, in the twelfth century, they were overthrown and supplanted by the Chauhān (Chāhamāna) Rajputs. Several temples, Hindu (Brāhmaṇical) and Jain, were erected during the Rajput rule. The Chauhān ruler, Prithvīrāja, was defeated by the Muslims towards the close of the twelfth century, and Delhi thus became the capital, initially of the Pathan Sultans and later of the Mughals. In the British period, when the country came under a unified control, initially the capital was at Calcutta, but it was shifted to Delhi in 1911. The independence of the country in 1947 did not interrupt that status.

With such a variegated history, it is not surprising that Delhi should abound in relics and remains of its long chequered past. The remains of its protohistoric and historic periods lie buried below later structures. Some idea of the life of people during these periods is provided by the antiquities and structural remains exposed at the Purana-Qila (p. 123). A glimpse of the Rajput art and architecture may be had from the reservoir of Sūraj-Kuṇḍ, ramparts and carved, though mutilated, pillars and ceiling-slabs of temples re-used by the early Muslims in Sultan Ghārī's tomb and the Quwwatu'l-Islām mosque. But it is the mosques, tombs and citadels of the Pathans and the Mughals that constitute the most monumental remains of Delhi. They are often spoken of as constituting seven cities.

Amongst more than thirteen hundred listed monuments of Delhi, about one hundred and forty are briefly described in this short guide. A visitor must select the monuments he wishes to visit according to his interest and the time at his disposal. Sūraj-Kuṇḍ, Tughluqabad, Qutb-Mīnār, Ḥauẓ-Khāṣ, Humāyūn's tomb, Purana-Qila, Safdar-Jang's tomb, Kotla Firoz Shāh and the Red Fort should perhaps figure even in a short itinerary; but if he must curtail it further, he must visit at least Sūraj-Kuṇḍ, Qutb-Minar and the Red Fort.

Most of the monuments described here are approachable by roads (pl. XXVII) and can be reached by bus or hired conveyance. The Delhi Transport Corporation runs two special services daily in winter, starting from the Scindia House in Cannaught Circus, one in the forenoon at 9.00 a.m. and the other in the afternoon at 2.15 p.m., covering a different set of monuments and other places of interest in each of its trips. In summer months there is only one long trip, the bus leaving at 7.30 a.m. For further details the visitor is advised to contact either the Infornation Officer of the Delhi Transport Corporation or the Tourist Office at 88 Janpath.

In a guide of this size, the descriptions have necessarily to be brief. A select bibliography is added at the end for the guidance of those who would like to study the monuments in some detail. The author has reproduced or adapted some of the material from his chapter on the Islamic monuments published in the *Archaeological Remains, Monuments and Museums* (New Delhi, 1964).

2. MAIN FEATURES OF INDO-ISLAMIC ARCHITECTURE

The conquest of India by the Muslims made an effective and distinct impact on the indigenous manifestations of life and culture, which gave rise, among other expressions of art, also to a new style in architecture. This style incorporated not only certain new modes and principles of construction but reflected also the religious and social needs of the adherents of Islam.

In the Hindu, Buddhist or Jain constructions, spaces were either spanned by beams, or the courses of bricks or stones were laid in corbels, so that the open span was gradually reduced to a size which could be covered with a single slab. Although there exists some evidence to suggest that the true arch may have been known in India earlier, the widely held belief is that the Muslims brought with them the principle of building a true arch, so that the bricks or stones could be laid as voussoirs to reproduce a curve and thus span the space between columns or walls. In any case, even if the true arch was familiar to indigenous architects in ancient times, it was re-introduced by the Muslims and firmly implanted on the soil. The result was that flat lintels or corbelled ceilings were replaced by arches or vaults and the pyramidal roof (*pīḍhā*) or spire (*śikhara*) by the dome. The necessity of raising a round dome over a square construction introduced multiplication of sides and angles by providing squinches, so that a base with many sides, usually sixteen, could be obtained to raise a circular drum for the dome. A sunshade or balcony was laid on cantilever brackets fixed into and projecting from the walls, which introduced the *chhajjā* (eaves or sunshade). Brackets with richly carved pendentives, described as stalactite pendentives, lent them fascinating ornamentation when they supported balconies. Kiosks (*chhatrīs*), tall towers (*mīnārs*) and half-domed double portals are some of the other distinguishing features of the Indo-Islamic architecture.

The difference in the lay-out of a temple and mosque is explained by the essential difference between the Hindu and Muslim forms of worship and prayer. A cella to house the image of the deity (*garbha-gṛiha*) and often a small hall in front for the worshippers (*maṇḍapa*) were regarded adequate for a simple Hindu temple. But the Islamic form of worship, with its emphasis on congregational prayer, requires a spacious courtyard (*ṣiḥn*) with a large prayer-hall at its western end (*liwān*). In the rear wall of the prayer-hall, the centre is occupied by a recess or alcove, called *miḥrāb*, and indicates the direction of prayer (*qibla*). A pulpit (*mimbar*) to its right is meant for the *imām* who leads the prayer. A tower or minaret, originally intended for the *mu'adhin* to call the faithful to the prayer (*ma'dhana*), later assumed merely an architectural character. A gallery or compartment is sometimes screened off in a corner of the prayer-hall or in some other part to accommodate the ladies who observed *purdah*. The main entrance to a mosque is on the east and the sides are enclosed by cloisters (*riwāqs*). A tank (*ḥauz*) is provided for ablutions usually in the courtyard of a mosque.

The practice of the burial of the dead, as distinct from cremation practised by the Hindus, introduced the tomb. A domed chamber (*ḥujra*) with a cenotaph (*ẓarīḥ*) in its centre, a *miḥrāb* in the western wall, and the real grave (*qabr*) in an underground chamber (*maqbara*) constitute the essential elements of a tomb. In larger and more complex tombs, there is also an independent mosque, and in later tombs a well-planned garden. The entrance to the mortuary-chamber is usually from the south.

The mode, theme or motifs of ornamentation empolyed in Islamic buildings are also different from the earlier Hindu vogues. The indigenous ornamentation is largely naturalistic, delineating with a conspicuous zest human and animal forms and the luxuriant vegetation-life characteristic of a tropical country. Among the Muslims the representation of living beings was forbidden by scriptural injunction, and so they took recourse to execution of geometrical and arabesque patterns, ornamental writing and a formal representation of plant and floral life, reflecting in its scantiness the nature of the country where Islam was born.

Lucidity and simplicity of expression, economic use of material and orderly arrangement of different parts characterize the Islamic art, as distinct from the exuberance, richness and exaggeration of the Hindu art. The ornamental designs in Islamic buildings were carved on stone in low relief, cut on plaster, painted or inlaid. Muslim ornamentation, even on stone or other base, in effect is usually close to embroidery. Striking colour effect was often obtained by encaustic enamel on tiles.

Lime was known earlier in India, but its use was very limited, mud being used for brickwork, while large blocks of stone were generally laid dry and secured to each other by means of iron clamps. The Muslims on the other hand made an extensive use of lime which served not merely as a binding-medium, but also as plaster and a base for incised decoration and encaustic enamel work.

After the initial reaction manifesting itself in the desecration, destruction and spoliation of the earlier Hindu structures the creative monumental activity of the Muslims is marked by two phases. In the first phase, the earlier Hindu temples or other buildings were purposefully demolished and the material used for new improvised buildings. In the later phase, mosques, tombs and other buildings were fully planned and built with appropriate material, which was originally quarried, manufactured or ornamented as necessary. It is in this phase that the Muslim buildings are found at their best.

Indo-Islamic architecture falls under three broad classes. The monuments erected by or under the patronage of the Sultans belong to the first class. Contemporaneously, at least in part, monuments were also coming up in the different provinces, which were originally ruled by governors appointed by the Sultans, but which soon declared themselves independent. These exhibit a diversified but distinct class. To the third class belong the constructions of the Mughals, who brought India under an almost united suzerainty.

The monuments in Delhi belong to the first and third class. While among important monuments of the first class there exist only two outside Delhi—the

Aṛhāi-Din-kā-Jhonpṛa at Ajmer and the Jāmi'-Masjid at Bari Khatu, District Nagaur—Delhi and Agra share between themselves the largest number of monuments erected by or associated with the Mughal rulers.

3. HISTORY AND ARCHITECTURE

A. Protohistoric Beginnings

The so-called seven cities of Delhi, the earliest of which may be dated to the closing years of the tenth century, are not all that Delhi has to offer as evidence of its past; neither do they cover the entire span of its long and eventful life. For habitation appears to have begun at or around the site of Delhi about three thousand years ago. Underneath the Purana-Qila, raised in the sixteenth century, trial trenching in 1955 revealed the occurrence of a fine grey earthenware, usually painted with simple designs in black. Known among the archaeologists as the Painted Grey Ware, this pottery is often dated to *c.* 1000 B.C. The site was systematically excavated during 1969-73, but a regular Painted Grey Ware horizon could not be located, although sherds of that ware were found in accumulations of a later age. A broad pattern can, however, be pieced together from the evidence available from certain other contemporary sites, which have been excavated on a larger scale.

It is significant that the Painted Grey Ware occurs at several places associated with the story of the great epic *Mahābhārata*, and one of these places, Indraprastha, capital of the Pāṇḍavas, is traditionally identified with Delhi. Significantly enough, a village by the name of Indarpat, which is obviously derived from the word Indraprastha, lay in the Purana-Qila itself till the beginning of the present century, when it was cleared along with other villages to make way for the capital of New Delhi to be laid out. The village of Sāravala (modern Sarban) in Delhi, from where a Sanskrit inscription of 1328 now lying in the Red Fort Museum was recovered (p. 15), is mentioned in the inscription itself as situated in the district (*pratigaṇa*) of Indraprastha[1].

According to the *Mahābhārata* the capital of the Kuru-country lay at Hastināpura on the banks of the Ganga, but when the relations between the Pāṇḍavas and their cousins Kauravas became strained, Dhṛitarāshṭra, the father of the latter, gave away the region of Khāṇḍavaprastha on the bank of the Yamuna to the former. There they 'measured out a city surrounded by ditches like the sea and provided with high defensive walls'. Apparently Indraprastha was this city, while the region in which it lay was known as Khāṇḍavaprastha. At the end of their victory over the Kauravas, the Pāṇḍavas are said to have returned to Hastināpura, and eventually to have handed over Indraprastha to a scion of the Yādava clan, to which Kṛishṇa, who had himself visited the Pāṇḍavas at Indraprastha, belonged.

There exists a tradition that the Pāṇḍavas had demanded from the Kauravas five villages, the names of which end in *pat*, the Hindi equivalent of Sanskrit *prastha*. These are said to be Indarpat, Baghpat, Tilpat,

[1] *Epigraphia Indica*, I (1892), pp. 93-95.

Sonepat and Panipat. The tradition is founded on the *Mahābhārata* sure enough, but the names of four villages mentioned there are different and the fifth one is left unnamed. Nevertheless, all the places named above, including Tilpat, which lies about 22 km south of Delhi on the eastern bank of the Okhla canal, have yielded the Painted Grey Ware.

In the settlements characterized by the presence of the Painted Grey Ware, iron and copper were used side by side. Other tools were made of bone, while clay, bone or glass was used to manufacture ornaments, such as beads and bangles. The inhabitants led essentially a pastoral-agricultural life. Their houses were built possibly of mud or wattle and daub.

B. Continuation from Early Historical to Medieval times

Evidence for habitation around Delhi from early historical to medieval times comes mainly from the excavations at Purana-Qila where the spade has cut through houses, soakwells and streets of the Sultanate, Rajput, Post-Gupta, Gupta, Śaka-Kushaṇ and Śuṅga days reaching down to the Maurya period. Evidence of the Maurya period (*c.* 300 B.C.) is provided by the occurrence of the Northern Black Polished Ware, a fine earthenware with a glossy surface, and punch-marked coins. Coins, characteristic pottery and terracotta sealings and figurines attest also to other periods named above.

Direct association of emperor Aśoka (273-36 B.C.) of the Maurya dynasty with Delhi has been brought to light only recently by the discovery of a shorter version of his Minor Rock Edicts engraved on a rock near Srinivaspuri.[1] This discovery also indicates that Delhi lay on the trunk route connecting the main cities of ancient India (p. 106).

There are also some other relics of historical times in Delhi, but they are not *in situ* and were much later imported from outside. Two of these are polished sandstone pillars inscribed with the edicts of Aśoka (pp. 26, 131, 136), which were brought here by Fīrūz S̲h̲āh Tug̲h̲luq (1351-88), and the third the well-known iron pillar in the Qutb area, manufactured in the Gupta period, but transplanted to Delhi perhaps in the tenth century (pp. 13, 55).

C. The Rajputs

It is from the Rajput period that monuments standing above the ground attract our attention, although houses of that period lying buried have also been uncovered at the Purana-Qila. Some beautifully sculptured sandstone lintels (pl.VA) and a railing-pillar mortised for crossbars were discovered some years ago embedded in the roof concrete of Sultan G̲h̲ārī's tomb, the earliest Muslim sepulchral monument of the Sultanate period built in the thirteenth century (pp. 19, 68). They may be dated to the seventh or eighth century, and provide an important clue to the existence of a large temple near Sultan G̲h̲ārī's tomb in early medieval days.

[1] M. C. Joshi and B. M. Pande, 'A newly-discovered inscription of Aśoka at Bahapur, Delhi,' *Journal of the Royal Asiatic Society of Great Britain and Ireland*, 1967, pts. 3-4, pp. 96-98.

It may have been erected by a feudatory of the Pratīhāras. These sculptures clearly indicate that the neighbourhood of Sultan Ghārī's tomb remained continuously inhabited at least from the early medieval times, as remains of pillars and *āmalaka*-slabs of a medieval date were already known from here. In fact, there might possibly be two main phases of pre-Muslim construction at Sultan Ghārī's tomb, a post-Gupta phase with use of red sandstone and a proper medieval one, when coarse grey or brownish sandstone and marble were used.

The Tomar Rajputs had established themselves in the Aravalli hills south of Delhi, originally probably as feudatories of the Pratīhāra rulers, at least from the closing years of the tenth century, if not earlier. An inscription of the early tenth century from Pehoa in Karnal District of Haryana names some Tomars as the builders of a triple temple.[1] They appear to have been in the employ of the king of Kanauj, but it is not certain if they had any relation with the Tomars of Delhi. Another inscription of the late tenth century from Harshanath in Sikar District also refers to them.[2] In any case, the bare and barren hills south of Delhi, isolated and difficult of access as they were, were apparently selected by the Tomars as a royal resort in preference to the plains, probably as they afforded a safe shelter from and were less exposed to the onslaughts of other hostile Rajput clans.

In these hills close to Delhi but within the present boundaries of Haryana, there are some important

[1] *Epigraphia Indica,* I (1892), pp. 242-50.
[2] *Ibid.,* II (1894), pp. 116-30.

constructions associable with the Tomars. Sūrajpāl, whose historicity is based more on bardic tradition than on other sources, is said to be the builder of the large reservoir, known as Sūraj-Kuṇḍ (pl. VI; p. 100). Over a kilometre to its south, close to the village of Aṛangpur, or Anangpur, is a dam ascribed to Anangpāl of the same dynasty (p. 101). Its neighbourhood is dotted with ruins of pavilions and fortifications, which lend some support to the popular belief that Aṛangpur is the successor of an earlier settlement founded by Anangpāl.

Anangpāl is, however, known in bardic tradition recorded in the *Pṛithvīrājarāso* as the founder of Delhi, although the tradition is perhaps not very old. He is said to have built the Lāl-Koṭ, which is the first known regular defence-work in Delhi and may be regarded as the core of the so-called first city of Delhi (p. 50). Anangpāl is also believed to have brought to Delhi and installed in the Lāl-Koṭ, the iron pillar (p. 55), which formed originally, as early as the fourth century, the standard of an unidentified Vishṇu temple.

King Vigraharāja IV (*c.* 1153-64), also known Viśāladeva or Bīsaldeo, of the Chāhamāna or Chauhān dynasty of Śākambharī (modern Sambhar), captured Delhi from the Tomars, perhaps soon after he came to power. An inscription of 1163 or 1164 on the Aśokan pillar, now in Kotla Firoz Shah, refers to Vigraharāja's conquest of the land between the Vindhyas and Himalayas.[1] His capture of Delhi is mentioned in an inscription from Bijolia in Udaipur District,[2] while other ins-

[1] *Indian Antiquary*, XIX (1890), pp. 215-19.
[2] *Epigraphia Indica*, XXVI (1841-42), pp. 84-113.

criptions refer to Delhi having been ruled successively by the Tomars and Chauhāns.[1] Vigraharāja's grandson Pṛithvīrāja III, also known as Rai Pithora, the popular hero of the stories of Hindu resistance against the Muslims, extended the Lāl-Koṭ by throwing up around it massive stone ramparts and gates, which go under the name of Qila Rai Pithora, the first city of Delhi.

The Tomars and Chauhāns built several temples within the Lāl-Koṭ, which were all pulled down by the Muslims and their stones re-utilized mainly in the Quwwatu'l-Islām mosque (p. 52). A four-armed stone image of Vishṇu (pl. V B), dated in *saṁvat* 1204 (A.D. 1147) was found recently to the south-east of the Qutb-Minar and is now exhibited in the National Museum. A long stone lintel, with scenes from the *Rāmāyaṇa* carved on both sides, was found some years ago on the outskirts of Haidarpur, 10 km north of Delhi, and may have been removed there from the Lāl-Koṭ area in later times, as no other contemporary relics are traceable at the site.

Pṛithvīrāja was ruling over Delhi when Muḥammad bin Sām of Ghūr led his incursions into India. The latter was repulsed at least once by a confederacy of the Rajputs under Pṛithvīrāja on the battle-field of Taraori. But next year, in 1192, a crushing defeat on the same battle-field was inflicted on Pṛithvīrāja, and he was killed. After this Muḥammad retired to his native land, leaving Quṭbu'd-Dīn Aibak, his slave, as his

[1] *Journal of the Asiatic Society of Bengal*, XLIII (1874), pp. 104-110; *Epigraphia Indica*, I (1892), pp. 93-95; *Ibid.*, XII (1913-14), pp. 17-27.

viceroy iṇ India. In 1193 Quṭbu'd-Dīn Aibak captured Delhi, which was still in the hands of the Chauhāns. Later, after the death of Muḥammad Ghūrī in 1206, he enthroned himself at Lahore as the first Sultan of Delhi. Delhi thus became the capital of the Mamlūk or Slave dynasty, the first dynasty of the Muslim Sultans to rule over the northern India.

D. Ancient names of Delhi

The first medieval city of Delhi, believed to have been founded by the Tomars, was called Ḍhillī or Ḍhillikā, although among the known records the name Ḍhillikā occurs for the first time in the inscription of 1170 from Bijolia, District Udaipur, referred to earlier, which mentions the capture of Delhi by the Chāhamānas. The Palam *Bāolī* inscription of 1276, written in the reign of Ghiyāthu'd-Dīn Balban, also calls the town Ḍhillī and the country in which it lies as Hariyānaka.[1] Another inscription dated in 1328 in the reign of Muḥammad Tughluq (1324-51), now in the Red Fort Museum,[2] also refers to the city of Ḍhillikā in the Hariyānā-country. A less-known inscription dated in 1316, found in Ladnu in District Didwana, also mentions the city of Dhillī in Harītāna country.[3] Evidently Delhi was an important town, and perhaps also the capital of Haryana. The modern name Delhi is derived from Dihlī or Dillī, the Hindi equivalent of Dhillī of the inscriptions. To

[1] *Journal of the Asiatic Society of Bengal*, XLIII (1874), pt. 1, pp. 104-10.
[2] *Epigraphia Indica*, I (1892), pp. 93-95.
[3] *Ibid.*, XII, pp. 17-27.

read in it *Dehalī*, the Hindi word for 'threshold', and to assert that Delhi signifies the threshold of the country, is only fanciful.

Another name, Yoginīpura, occurs as an alternative of Dhillī in the Palam *Bāolī* inscription, which also mentions the village of Pālamba, obviously the modern Palam. Both Dhillī and Yoginīpura occur frequently in Jain *Pāttāvalīs*. A king by the name of Madanapāla is mentioned as ruling over Dhillī or Yoginīpura in *saṁvat* 1223 (A.D. 1166).[1] Since the words *madana* and *anaṅga* are synonymous in Sanskrit, there is some likelihood that the king under reference may be Anangpāl, the date given being a mistake. The Jain literary tradition gains some support from the fact that Delhi was obviously also an important Jain centre in medieval days, as evidenced by several Jain sculptures found re-used in the Quwwatu'l-Islām mosque The name Yoginīpura is believed to owe its origin to a temple of *yoginīs* ('female semi-divine beings'), which exists no longer but the memory of which is preserved in the present Jogamāyā temple (p. 60) near Mehrauli, which itself ss derivable from 'Mihirapurī, and suggests that a sun-temple may have also existed here.

E. The Delhi Sultanate (1206-1526)

Delhi turned a new leaf in its history from the date of its capture by Quṭbu'd-Dīn Aibak. The whole pattern of its life felt the impact of the culture and faith of the invaders and continued to experience it for the next six

[1] *Kharataragahchchha-Bṛhadgurvāvalī*, Bombay, 1956, pp. 21-22.

centuries and a half. The new culture manifested itself no less in architecture than in other expressions of art. The remains of numerous buildings raised during this long period are frequently grouped as the seven cities of Delhi. But it is a 'misleading description which the visitor finds hard to reconcile with a landscape strewn haphazard with a thousand mosques, forts, tombs, walls and incomprehensible ruined structures, few of which seem to fall into any coherent plan suggesting a city.' The monuments present, however, a grand panorama, interrupted though it is by the equally haphazard present expansion of the city and its suburbs, and illustrate two of the three main classes of Indo-Islamic architecture (p. 7).

Five dynasties ruled from Delhi from the assumption of power by Quṭbu'd-Dīn Aibak till its conquest by the Mughals. The rule of these dynasties of Sultans is distributed into the following periods:

1.	Slave or Mamlūk dynasty, including Balban and his successors	1206-1290
2.	Khaljī dynasty	1290-1321
3.	Tughluq dynasty	1321-1414
4.	Sayyid dynasty	1414-1444
5.	Lodī dynasty	1451-1526

(i) *Slave or Mamlūk Dynasty*

Quṭbu'd-Dīn declared himself Sultan in 1206, but he had commenced his architectural career earlier in 1193 when he conquered Delhi and was appointed as viceroy by Muhammad Ghūrī. In their iconoclastic zeal the conquerors laid the Hindu temples in Delhi waste. They aimed to raise in their place their own buildings on the principles of construction followed by them in their homeland but were confronted with the lack of workmen familiar with their methods. The result was that a sense of uncertainty and improvisation permeated through the buildings of the Slave dynasty, some of which were, in fact, built with architectural pieces from demolished Hindu temples. The indigenous use of architrave, lintel or corbelled courses continued in their earlier buildings; and, in fact, the hand of Hindu craftsmen used to naturalistic motifs is particularly apparent in surface-ornamentation. Although a homogenous principle of construction and ornamentation was lacking in these buildings, the product was often marked by grace and strength rooted in the soil.

The Tomar citadel of Lāl-Koṭ, which with its later Chauhān extension into Qila Raí Pithora is known as the first city of Delhi, was occupied by Quṭbu'd-Dīn. He demolished here twenty-seven Hindu and Jain temples, and with their carved columns, lintels, ceiling-slabs and other members completed in 1198 the Quwwatu'l-Islām ('might of Islam') mosque, enclosing a rectangular area with cloisters on the sides (pl. VIII). Later he added an imposing screen with lofty arches in front of the prayer-chamber on the west (pl. VII). The arches are built with corbelled courses, although there is a faint attempt to lay the stones in the fashion of voussoirs near the apex of the arches. The hand of Hindu craftsmen is clearly perceptible in the ornamentation of the screen, not only with its serpentine tendrils and undulating leaves but also in the curves of the characters of the Quranic inscriptions.

In the final year of the twelfth century, Quṭbu'd-Dīn laid the foundation of the Qutb-Minar, (pls. IX and X A ; p. 53), the tallest stone-tower in India, 72·5m in height. Possibly raised both as a tower of victory and as a *mīnār* attached to the mosque for the *mu'adhin* to call the faithful to the prayer, it was completed by Quṭbu'd-Dīn's successor and son-in-law, Shamsu'd-Dīn Iltutmish (1211-36), who also enlarged the mosque, including its screen. The arches of his screen are still corbelled, although their arabesque ornamentation is Saracenic, as distinct from the mixed decoration of Quṭbu'd-Dīn's screen. His square tomb (p. 56), with its dome no longer in existence, is profusely carved on the inside with inscriptions and geometrical designs, recalling in its richness the Hindu ideal of ornamentation but almost fully Saracenic in detail, except some of the motifs which may have been derived from Hindu tradition. Iltutmish had also built in 1231 a tomb for his eldest son and heir-apparent, prince Nāṣiru'd-Dīn, who died in 1228-29 during the life-time of his father. Known as Sultan Ghārī's tomb, from its crypt-chamber (Persian *ghār*), it is the earliest existing monumental Muslim tomb, excepting some pre-Sultanate tombs in District Kutch, and was constructed with architectural pieces from demolished Hindu temples. The construction of its arches and vaults is still corbelled, while the ceilings of its chamber and corridors are built with columns, brackets and beams

Iltutmis͟h had nominated his daughter Raziya to succeed him, but the courtiers put his eldest surviving son Ruknu'd-Dīn Fīrūz on the throne. He reigned for about six months, when his subjects rebelled and crowned the princess in 1236 as the first and only woman Sultan to ascend the throne to Delhi. She was killed in 1240 at Kaithal in District Karnal, and a grave there is pointed out as containing her bodily remains. On the other hand, an unroofed stone-walled enclosure within the later city of S͟hāhjahānābād in Delhi is believed by many to contain her real grave (p. 144).

Nāṣiru'd-Dīn, the last Sultan in Quṭbu'd-Dīn's line, was fanatically religious and did not care much for the affairs of state, which were left by him to Ulug͟h K͟hān Balban, originally one of Iltutmis͟h's slaves and now Nāṣiru'd-Dīn's father-in-law and minister. In the absence of an heir, Balban (1265-87) succeeded Nāṣiru'd Dīn. His dynasty came to an abrupt end in 1290, after two successors had ruled after him.

Although a palace is ascribed to Balban in Delhi, it has not yet been identified. An unassuming rubble-built square tomb, not far from the Qutb-Minar, now dilapidated and domeless, is, however, believed to be his tomb and is the first Muslim monument where true arch was employed for the first time.

About 1287 Balban's successor, Mu'izzu'd-Dīn Kaiqubād, shifted his capital to Kilokaṛī on the bank of the Yamuna. Lying in the neighbourhood of the present Jamia Milia Islamia, close to the headworks of the Okhla Canal, this capital is now survived only by some mounds and lonely structures.

(*ii*) *Khaljī Dynasty*

Fīrūz Shāh, an Afghanized Turk of the Khaljī tribe at the Delhi court, captured the throne in 1290 from Shamsu'd-Dīn Kaimurth, the last king in Balban's line, and assumed the title of Jalālu'd-Dīn Khaljī. Among the six rulers of Khaljī dynasty, the third in the line, Alāu'd-Dīn, ascended the throne in 1296 and is well-known, not only for his political exploits, but also for his architectural ambitions and achievements. This was just the time when the empire of the Saljuqs in western Asia was breaking up under the incessant inroads of the Mongols, and the poets, artists, architects and craftsmen under their employ were taking shelter in neighbouring lands. Some of them, no doubt, resorted to the Delhi court, and brought with them Saljuqian architectural traditions, which resulted in such characteristics in Khaljī buildings as the 'lotus-bud' fringe on the underside of the arch, apparently mistakenly described as a 'spear-head' fringe, ornamental bosses in relief in spandrels and alternating courses of narrow 'headers' and wide 'stretchers' in the masonry-face. The initial phase of experimentation and improvisation in Islamic architecture was now over, and it developed its own methods and idioms. Employment of true arch, mostly in the form of a pointed horseshoe, broad dome, recessed arches under the squinch, perforated windows, decorative mouldings, arabesque low reliefs, inscriptional bands and use of red sandstone relieved by marble are some of the other features which characterize the Khaljī architecture.

'Alāu'd-Dīn extended the Quwwatu'l-Islām mosque in Delhi by enlarging its enclosure and the screen. Among its gateways built by him only the southern one, called the 'Alā'ī Darwāza, has survived in entirety (pl. XI A). The 'lotus-bud' fringe on the underside of a horseshoe-shaped arch appeared here for the first time, and the monotone of red stone was relieved by inscribed marble bands (pl. X B). He also commenced building another *mīnār* within the extended Quwwatu'l-Islām mosque, but had hardly raised the tower to its first storey when death overtook him. He had doubled the size of the mosque, and his *mīnār* was also intended to be twice the size of the Qutb-Minar. The *Tārīkh-i-'Alāhī* of Amīr Khusraw states that 'Alāu'd-Dīn ordered that the old *mīnār* was to be provided with a casing and cupola.[1] One of the Nāgarī inscriptions on the *mīnār* certainly indicates that 'Alāu'd-Dīn carried out some repairs to the tower, as it describes the *mīnār* as 'Alāu'd-Dīn's victory-tower (*vijaya-stambha*).[2] He died in 1316 and a building to the south-west of the mosque is believed to comprise his tomb and a *madrasa* or college raised by him.

In 1303 'Alāu'd-Dīn laid the foundations of Sīrī, which was the second city of Delhi but the first to be originally built by the Muslims. It is represented now only by stretches of its thick stone walls provided with 'flame'-shaped battlements, which appeared here for the first time. He also dug the vast reservoir at Hauz-

[1] H. M. Illiot, *The History of India as told by its own historians*, Vol. III, Allahabad, p. 70.
[2] M. C. Joshi, 'Some Nāgarī inscriptions on the Qutb Minar', *Medieval India-A Miscellany*, Aligarh, Vol. 2, p. 3.

Khās, which was originally known as Ḥauz-i-'Alā'ī and was intended to meet the needs of the citizens of Sīrī.

During 'Alāu'd-Dīn reign his son Khizr Khān is said to have built the Jamā'at-Khāna-Masjid, which lies close to the tomb of Hazrat Niẓāmu'd-Dīn Auliya. Its red sandstone facing, low dome, the 'lotus-bud' fringe of arches, recessed squinch-arches, frames of Quranic inscriptions and the arrangement of alternating wide and narrow courses are features which all recall the 'Alā'l-Darwāza.

(iii) *Tughluq Dynasty*

The last of the Khaljīs, 'Alāu'd-Dīn's third son, Quṭbu'd-Dīn Mubārak Khān, was killed by Khusraw Khān, a low caste Hindu convert in the Sultan's favour, who had been appointed as his chief minister by him. Ghāzī Malik, a Turk nobleman of Tughluq tribe, who was then governor of Debalpur in Puṇjab and whose loyalty to his Khaljī overlords was unbounded, marched against Khusraw Khān and beheaded him. There being no male survivor from the house of the Khaljīs, he was proclaimed king in 1321 under the title of Ghiyāthu'd-Dīn Tughluq, popularly known as Tughluq Shāh.

Among the eleven rulers from the Tughluq dynasty, only the first three were interested in architecture, and each added a new capital-city in Delhi. Under the Khaljīs architecture had begun to acquire a standard proportion of mass, grace and ornament and a preference for an appropriate use of red colour to relieve the grey, drab surfaces. But with the puritanical Tughluqs the order changed. Their buildings are distinguished by plain and austere surfaces of grey stone, cross-vaults over large halls, battered walls and bastions, the latter particularly on the quoins, four-centred arches and lintels above the openings. Battered construction, a necessity in thick walls of mud or bricks, but not in stone, may have been borrowed by the Tughluqs from Sind, Punjab or even Afghanistan, where mud or brick was in use.

The element of reduced ornament in the Tughluq buildings frequently shows them to an advantage. Inscribed borders and medallions in spandrels, often executed on plaster or stucco, obtain an extremely effective result. The drab look of the plain mass was further relieved by encaustic tiles, which appear to have been introduced in the Tughluq period for the first time. The Tughluqs were also interested in impounding rain water for irrigation by erecting bunds and embankments, and some of these have survived to this day.

Ghiyāthu'd-Dīn Tughluq (1321-25) built the fortified town of Tughluqabad, the third city of Delhi (p. 101). With its battered walls of grey rubble perched on desolate hills (pl. XII A), where its position gives it a natural advantage, Tughluqabad, with its city and citadel, was raised as a stronghold rather than as a metropolis with architectural ambitions. Across its main entrance on the south is Ghiyāthu'd-Dīn tomb (pl. XII B; p. 102), a red sandstone building relieved by a restrained use of marble and enclosed within a rubble-built fortress-like irregular pentagon. With a 'lotus-bud' fringe on the underside of its arched openings on three sides and its colour-scheme, it still retains some of the characteristics of the Khaljī architecture, although it has also introduced new features like the arched with an ogee-curve at the apex resembling the 'Tudor' arch, a slightly-pointed 'Tartar' dome and the use of beam-and-arch for openings. Originally this fortress-tomb stood within a vast artificial reservoir of rain water, impounded by joining the spurs of hills with embankments and was connected with Tughluqabad by a causeway, now pierced by the Qutb-Badarpur toad.

Ghiyāthu'd-Dīn's successor Muḥammad bin Tughluq (1325-51) added the small fortress of 'Ādilābād (p. 104) on the hills south of Tughluqabad, with which it shares the main characteristics of construction. He also raised the fourth city of Delhi, Jahānpanāh (p. 73), which largely comprised a walled enclosure between Qila Rai Pithora and Sīrī in order to afford protection to his subjects living there. Tughluqabad, however, continued to be the main city, and it was from here that Muḥammad transferred not merely the capital but also the entire population of Delhi to Daulatabad in the Deccan, and later brought them back again.

The next ruler Fīrūz Shāh (1351-88), who was fond of history, hunting, irrigation and architecture, founded several towns. In and around Delhi, apart from raising new buildings, he also repaired old ones, such as Sultan Ghārī's tomb (p. 69), Qutb-Minar (p. 54) and Sūraj-Kuṇḍ (p. 100). Series of low domes over mosques and stone railings around a terrace or open courtyard are some of the new architectural features introduced in his reign. The two inscribed Aśokan columns, one at Topra near Ambala and the other near Meerut, then undeciphered, excited his curiosity, and were brought by him and erected in Delhi, the former in his new capital (p. 131) and the latter on the ridge (p. 136), near his hunting-palace, known as Pīr-Ghaib.

His new capital, called Fīrūzābād, the fifth city of Delhi, the citadel-quadrangles of which are now known as Kotla Firoz Shāh, is a large enclosure of high walls, along which then flowed the river. With an entrance through a barbicaned main gate on the west, it contained palaces, pillared halls, mosques, a pigeon-tower and a *bāolī*, some of which are still in good condition. Among these the tall pyramidal structure supporting the Aśokan pillar and the Jāmi'-Masjid (p. 130) were famed far and wide in the contemporary times. The fact that the capital was moved to the riverside suggests that the Muslim power was now strongly established and enjoyed a considerable measure of prosperity, which necessitated the use of river for transport and communication.

Fīrūz Shāh built several hunting-lodges in and around Delhi, some of which, such as Mālcha-Mahal (p. 96), Bhūlī-Bhaṭiyārī-kā-Mahal (p. 96) and Pīr-Ghāib (p. 135) lie on the ridge. His other interest was irrigation. Ḥauz-i-'Alā'ī, a large reservoir which was built earlier by 'Alāu'd-Dīn Khaljī and which now lay in ruins, was restored by him, and on its south-western corner were built long halls in two storeys to serve as a *madrasa* or college (pl. XIV B; p. 79). This place, now known as Hauz-Khas, includes his tomb, a lofty structure with an impressive dome. Another embankment built by him is found at Mahipalpur (p. 70), where also he raised a hunting-palace.

Fīrūz Shāh's reign witnessed several mosques in Delhi. Khān-i-Jahān Jūnān Shāh, son of Maqbūl Khān, the father also bearing the title of Khān-i-Jahān, who was a Hindu convert and became prime minister of Fīrūz Shāh, is credited with building seven mosques, among which Kālī-or Kalān-Masjid within the city near Turkman Gate (p. 143), another mosque of the same name in Nizamuddin (p. 118), Khiṛkī-Masjid (pl. XV; p.-75), and Begampurī-Masjid (pl. XIX A; p. 71) are well-known. The two Kālī-Masjids bear inscriptions and are definitely built by the son; whether the builder of others is the father or the son is not certain. All these mosques are characterized by eaves or *chhajjas,* low domes and sloping *mīnārs* on corners and at the entrance. The courtyards of the Khiṛkī- and Kālī-Masjids, the latter situated in Nizamuddin, are divided into squares, some roofed and others left uncovered to admit light.

The tomb of Khān-i-Jahān Tilangānī (p. 118), who is obviously no other than Maqbūl Khān, Fīrūz Shāh's prime minister himself, also lies in Nizamuddin. It consists of a domed octagonal chamber enclosed by a verandah, each of its sides pierced by three arches. It is the first octagonal tomb in Delhi, some earlier ones although with a different pattern, having been built in Multan. Later this style became the hallmark of Sayyid and Lodī architecture.

After the death of Fīrūz Shāh Tughluq in 1388, the Sultanate became politically unstable. In 1396, Nusrat

Shāh, one of Fīrūz Shāh's grandsons, usurped the throne from Maḥmūd Tughluq, although the latter managed to return to the throne in 1399 after Nuṣrat Shāh's murder. Tīmūr Lane invaded India in 1398 and plundered and devastated the town of Delhi mercilessly. He retreated next year, but the country could not recover for a long time, with nobles and provincial governors warring against each other and against the Sultan. With this kind of political unstability and the long-lasting effects of Tīmūr's invasion, the architectural activities came almost to a dead-stop.

(*iv*) *Sayyid Dynasty*

After Maḥmūd Tughluq's death in 1413, the courtiers transferred their allegiance to Daulat Khān Lodī, who was attacked and taken prisoner by Khiẓr Khān, governor of Punjab, in 1414. Khiẓr Khān ascended the throne and founded the Sayyid dynasty. Four rulers of this dynasty reigned in succession till 1444, but the country knew no prosperity. There was no patronization of arts or architecture. No cities, palaces or mosques were built, as happened during the rule of earlier dynasties. Only tombs were raised to shelter the dead, as if to match with the prevailing macabre atmosphere.

Yet some of these tombs are architecturally of no mean value. They are of two designs, octagonal and square. The former style had made a beginning during the Tughluq period with the tomb of Khān-i-Jahān Tilangānī (p. 118). The latter came to have a distinct elevation, with the façade broken up by a string-course and with series of panels of sunk niches above and below it giving it the semblance of two or three 'storeys'. In these tombs the central portion of each side projects to form a vertical rectangle, within which the main arch, with a beam-and-bracket entrance and a small open window above it, covers almost the entire height of the wall. The sides of the rectangle and corners of the structure are provided with pinnacles (*guldastas*). One arch on either side of the entrance is open or provided with latticed screen to admit light, but the others, like those on the second 'storey', are false and closed. These square tombs are higher than the octagonal ones, although the latter cover a wider area on the ground plan.

Unfortunately the persons buried in most of these square tombs remain unidentified, and there exists an impression that they contain the remains of noblemen, while the kings were buried in octagonal ones. On the other hand, it seems likely that the square plan became popular in the Lodī period, as the first inscribed tomb of this design, the tomb of Mubārak Khān, popularly known as Kāle Khān-kā-Gumbad (p. 86), is dated to 1481 during the Lodī rule.

Khiẓr Khān's son and successor, Mu'izzu'd-Dīn Mubārak Shāh is said to have founded a city called Mubārakābād along the Yamuna, but no trace of it now remains. He died in 1434, and lies buried in Kotla Mubarakpur (p. 87). His tomb, octagonal on plan, with a central chamber and verandahs around it, each side pierced by three openings, is typical of this style, although somewhat stunted with its wide dome and sloping buttresses on the corners in the Tughluq style.

The tomb of Muḥammad S͟hāh, who died in 1444, lies in the Lodi Gardens (p. 91). Although built on an octagonal plane, it has a raised drum, and so is the height of its *chhatrīs*, with the result that it looks much more impressive than Mubārak S͟hāh's tomb.

(*v*) *Lodī Dynasty*

During the reign of Muḥammad S͟hāh Sayyid (1434-44), Buhlūl Lodī, the Afghan governor of Sirhind, had extended his influence through Punjab and had become almost independent. 'Alāu'd-Dīn 'Ālam S͟hāh, Muḥammad S͟hāh's son and successor, returned to Budaun, leaving the governorship of Delhi to one brother-in-law and the superintendence of the city-police to another. The two, however, fell apart, and in 1451 Buhlūl Lodī captured the throne, although initially he professed to reign on behalf of 'Ālam S͟hāh.

Buhlūl (1451-89) brought some kind of order on the political scene but was engaged largely in subduing the provincial governor of Jaunpur and other chiefs. His successors, Sikandar and Ibrāhīm, remained likewise occupied. Under such circumstances there existed no impetus for raising new buildings; and all that the Lodīs have left are some tombs, in the two styles that had come into vogue during the Sayyid period. The simplest octagonal tomb is an open pillared pavilion, and a large number of them are found all over Delhi. But even the elaborate design continued to be followed till the reign of Akbar, although by then the royal tombs had come to have a different design. There are several tombs of the square variety in Delhi, a large number of them scattered between Hauz-Khās and Zamrudpur, but the identity of the persons buried in them is not known. The Shīsh-Gumbad in the Lodī Gardens follows the pattern described earlier (p. 28). It was decorated with glazed tiles, from which it derives its present name, meaning the 'dome of glass' (p. 93).

Buhlūl Lodī's tomb in Chiragh-Delhi falls in a class apart. It is an ordinary square structure, each side broken by three arched openings and the roof surmounted by five domes (p. 78). Sikandar (1489-1517) lived largely at Agra and raised some buildings at the place which acquired from him the name of Sikandara. During his reign in 1501 was built in Delhi Shihābu'd-Dīn Khān's tomb, known as Bāgh-i-'Ālam-kā-Gumbad, which follows the usual norm of square tombs (p. XVI A; p. 81). It is, however, his tomb in Delhi (pl. XVI B; p. 94) which exemplifies the final phase in the evolution of the octagonal tomb. The tomb proper possesses the same feature, as Muhammad Shāh's tomb. It stands, however, within a large square garden enclosed by high walls, provided with a wall mosque on the west and an ornamental entrance on the south. The mosque and square garden enclosure are features which later became characteristic of the Mughal tombs.

Two mosques built in Delhi during the rule of the Lodīs deserve mention, as certain features, which developed into important characteristics in the Mughal period, are found introduced here for the first time. The prayer-chamber of the Baṛā-Gumbad mosque in the Lodi Gardens, built in 1484, is divided into five bays and is surmounted by three domes, resting on corbelled pendentives, the end-bays being roofed by low vaults (pl. XVII; p. 92). It is richly ornamented with foliage and inscriptions in stucco and coloured titles. Oriel windows project at its rear from the ends and the centre; and the external angles and the *miḥrāb* bay are strengthened by sloping buttresses. Making the horizontal arm of a L-shape with it is an imposing domed tomb now known as Baṛā-Gumbad, which has 'double-storeyed' façades. Its position and the fact that no grave now exists in this chamber has misled some scholars to believe that this structure was raised as a gateway to the mosque.

The Moṭh-Masjid built by Miyān Bhuwa, a minister of Sikandar Lodī, is raised from a platform faced with cells. Its prayer-chamber surmounted by three domes is also faced with five graceful arched openings, the central one being the highest, and each fitted with tiled medallions in the spandrels. Like the Baṛā-Gumbad mosque, it has sloping buttresses flanking the rear projection, double-storeyed corner-towers and oriel windows (pl. XIX; p. 78).

F. The Sūrs and the Mug͟hals (1526-1707)

During the later part of his reign Ibrāhīm Lodī (1517-26) became particularly suspicious and capricious, not hesitating even to maltreat or imprison his nobles and provincial governors, with the result that there was always someone among them in rebellion against him. Bābur, the Mug͟hal king of Kabul, had already raided India twice, but now Daulat K͟hān

Lodī, governor of Lahore, who was much too discontented with the Delhi Sultan, sent Bābur an invitation to attack the Sultan. Bābur entered India in 1523 but had to go back owing to the pressure of the Uzbeks on Balkh. In 1526 he returned, and the armies of Ibrāhīm and Bābur met at the famous battle of Panipat. Ibrāhīm was killed and Bābur occupied Delhi and Agra. A vast kingdom in India thus came under the Mug͟hals.

During the rule of the Sayyids and Lodīs, all cultural activity, including art and architecture had begun showing signs of stagnation, the new constructions being limited to tombs. The Sūrs and Mug͟hals infused fresh blood into this situation and raised architecture once again to its pinnacles, which was due largely to their personal interest and patronage, but also to the comparatively peaceful times and general prosperity under them. When, however, the personal interest of the sovereign waned, as happened during the rule of the later Mug͟hals, aesthetic appreciation and architectural enterprise abruptly declined. Delhi and Agra, which now occupied the position of capitals alternatey, were enriched handsomely by the Mug͟hals by construction of new buildings, as will be clear from the following account.

(*i*) *Bābur* (*1526-30*)

Bābur was a man of culture and exceptional aesthetic taste. He was particularly fond of formal gardens, and at least two gardens are believed to have been laid by him, one at Agra and the other at Panipat. He was not much impressed by the Indian workmen, yet in his

Memoirs he gives the number of stone-cutters and artisans engaged on his buildings, from which it appears possible that some of the monuments raised by him have not survived. There are very few buildings which are known to have been built either by him or under his direct patronage. These are the Kābulī-Bāgh mosque at Panipat, the Jāmi'-Masjid at Sambhal, a mosque at Ayodhya and a mosque within the Lodī fort at Agra, which finds mention in his *Memoirs*.

Falling within his reign is, however, a small brick-built mosque with three arched openings at Palam (p. 70), near Delhi. The much more ambitious and refined mosque of Jamālī-Kamālī in Mehraulī was also commenced about the same time, but completed during Humāyūn's reign (p. 66).

(*ii*) *Sūr Dynasty* (*1540-55*)

Bābur conquered India but did not consolidate his territory. After his death in Agra in 1530, his son, Humāyūn, succeeded him, only to face trouble from Sher Shāh, whose grandfather Ibrāhīm Khān, an Afghan from Sūr, had entered the service of Bahlūl Lodī and who had himself served under Bābur. He was now up in arms against Hamāyūn, and, in 1540, drove him from India, obliging him to take shelter in Iran. Sher Shāh met his end in 1545, but the Sūr dynasty continued to reign till 1555, when Humāyūn returned, overthrew Sikandar Shāh Sūr, then ruling, and regained his throne.

Sher Shāh was not only a man of exceptional courage and a great administrator but was also devoted to learning and intellectual pursuits. He improved the communications by constructing several roads, providing them with trees, mosques, wells and sarais at regular intervals, and posting horses at different stages to carry the royal mail. Among these, the main trunk road from the Indus to Sonargaon in Bengal, passing through Lahore, Delhi and Agra, and following the alignment bequeathed by it to the present Grand Trunk Road, is best known. He also built several forts, tombs and mosques.

The monuments built by Sher Shāh during his early career lie outside Delhi, such as at Sasaram and Narnaul, where he had spent his childhood and adolescent days. After his enthronement he concentrated his building activities at Delhi, which may be described as the second phase of the Sūr architecture. To begin with, he appears to have razed to the ground the city of Dīnpanāh built by Humāyūn. Later, on an adjacent site, which was earlier perhaps the site of Indraprastha, capital of the Pāṇḍavas (p. 9), he raised the citadel of Purana-Qila, the sixth city of Delhi, with the general town sprawling around it except on the east where the Yamuna flowed. Irregularly oblong on plan, with three gateways, high embattled walls and bastions, it lies picturesquely on the ancient elevated mound. The city of Sher Shāh around his citadel was extensive, two points on its circumference being perhaps provided by the so-called Sher Shāh's gate (p. 128) to the west of the Purana-Qila and the Kābulī- or Khūni-Darwāza (p. 132) to the west of Kotla Firoz Shah on the Delhi-Mathura road.

The Qal'a-i-Kuhna-Masjid (pl. XVIII A; p. 126), better known as Sher Shāh's mosque, inside the Purana-

Qila, which served as Chapel Royal, marks a step forward from the Moṭh-Masjid. It is, on one hand, anticipatory of the mosque design, as it took shape in the early Mughal period, and, on the other, emphasizes the ornate phase of Sher Shāh's architecture, as distinct from the plain treatment and earlier tradition noticed in the tombs raised by him at Narnaul and Sasaram. Its prayer-hall, surmounted by a dome flanked by *chhatrīs*, now missing, is faced by five openings with pointed arches, inclining towards the four-centred form. The central arch, fringed with lotus-cusps, is framed within decorative bands of inscriptions and geometrical designs, with thin side-pilasters. The niches of the western wall are also richly decorated. The *miḥrābs* are uniquely designed, by sinking one arch within another. Oriel windows, a narrow gallery on the second storey and semi-octagonal three-storeyed towers on rear-corners are some of its other interesting features. The Sher-Manḍal in its neighbourhood (p. 127), a double-storeyed octagonal tower of red stone relieved by marble, was perhaps originally intended as a pleasure-tower, although it is believed to have been used by Humāyūn as his library, from the stairs of which he fell down and died.

The successors of Sher Shāh had no particular interest in architecture. The fortress of Salīmgaṛh (p. 148) adjoining the Red Fort is believed to have been built by Sher Shāh's son, Islām Shāh (1545-54), also known as Salīm Shāh. During his reign in 1547 was also built, close to where Humāyūn's tomb was sited later, the octagonal tomb of 'Īsā Khān (pl. XI B; p. 111), a

nobleman at S͟her S͟hāh's court, who also served Islām
S͟hāh after the former's death.

(iii) Humāyūn (1530-40 and 1555-56)

Humāyūn ascended the throne in 1530 but was
pushed out of the country in 1540 by S͟her S͟hāh Sūr, as
mentioned earlier (p. 34). During this reign of ten years, he
was continuously engaged in warfare with the provincial
governors in addition to the pressure exerted by S͟her
S͟hāh. In these circumstances, he had no leisure, nor
any enthusiasm, for intellectual or cultural pursuits, including architecture. He returned to throne in July 1555,
after defeating Sikandar S͟hāh Sūr, but died in January
1556, which gave him no time even for consolidation
of his vast empire, much less for other activities. His
addiction to drugs also must have sapped him off his
verve and industry conducive to such artistic activities.

Yet his reign is not entirely barren. In 1533 he laid
the foundations of Dīnpanāh, a new city, on the bank
of the Yamuna in Delhi, and it was completed, with its
walls, bastions and gates, within the short period of ten
months, with the building material robbed from 'Alāu'd
Dīn's Sīrī. Humāyūn took considerable pains in selecting
the site of Dīnpanāh and laid its foundations in the
presence of his nobles and elders at an hour prescribed
as propitious by the learned and astrologers. But no trace
of it now remains, as it was pulled down systematically
by S͟her S͟hāh Sūr.

After regaining his throne, Humāyūn is said to have
completed parts of the Purana-Qila left unfinished by

Sher Shāh. During his reign was, however, completed at Mehrauli, the Jamālī-Kamālī-Masjid (p. 66), which was commenced in about 1528-29 during his father's reign. Jamālī was the *nom de plume* of Shaikh Faẓlu'llāh, a poet, whose tomb, profusely ornamented with glazed tiles and cut plaster lies next to the mosque. Surmounted by a single high dome, with its five recessed niches on the western wall, oriel windows at the back, octagonal towers at the rear-corners and a staircase leading to a narrow gallery on the second storey, it has an important place in the evolution of the Mughal mosque, for it contains features both of Moṭh-Masjid (pp. 32, 78) and Baṛā-Gumbad-Masjid (pp. 31, 92), built earlier, and of Sher Shāh's mosque (pp. 35, 126), built later.

As mentioned earlier (p. 36), the Sher-Manḍal in Purana-Qila is believed to have been used by Humāyūn as his library. As he was descending, he heard the call of the *mu'adhdhin* and seated himself down immediately on the steps. When he got up, his feet slipped and he fell down, the injuries ultimately bringing about his end in 1556. His senior widow, Bega Begam, also known as Hājī Begam, commenced his tomb (pl. I; p. 107) in 1565, nine years after his death. It is the first distinct example of the proper Mughal style, which is inspired by Persian architecture. There need be no doubt that Humāyūn picked up ideas of Persian architecture during his exile; he himself is likely to have planned the tomb, although there is no record to that effect. The square double-storeyed mausoleum built of red sandstone, with three arched alcoves on each side.

rises over a terrace, in the centre of a garden divided into four main parterres by shallow channels (chahārbāgh) The octagonal central chamber contains the cenotaph, while the corner-chambers house the graves of other members of the royal family. Over the roof, pillared kiosks are disposed around its high emphatic double dome, which occurs here for the first time in India.

The mausoleum is a synthesis of Persian architecture and Indian traditions—the former exemplified by the arched alcoves, corridors and the high double dome, and the latter by the kiosks, imparting it a pyramidal profile and by such features as use of beam and lintel in *dālāns*. Although Sikandar Lodī's tomb was the first garden-tomb to be built in India, it is Humāyūn's tomb which set up a new vogue, the crowning achievement of which is the Tāj-Mahal at Agra. There is also a somewhat common human impetus behind these two edifices: one is erected by a devoted wife for her husband and the other by an equally or more devoted husband for his wife.

(*iv*) *Akbar* (*1556-1605*)

At the death of Humāyūn, his elder son Akbar was only thirteen, and during his early years of rule, his tutor Bairam Khān acted as the regent. Akbar resisted verbal tuitioning and remained almost illiterate but acquired a spirit of universal toleration and liberality of outlook. Later in life he participated in theological debates between various sects of Islam and listened even to the teachings of the religions. In fact, he tried to promulgate a faith of his own, the Dīn-i-Ilāhī ('Divine Faith'). His relations with the Hindus were most cordial, and he married the Hindu princess of Amber, as also other Rajput princesses and permitted them to lead their Hindu life at home. Among his trusted Hindu courtiers were Raja Mān Singh of Amber and Raja Todar Mal. He was keenly interested in art and architecture. The Mug͟hal style of painting developed under his guidance, as a result of fusion of Hindu and Persian techniques. His architecture is characterized equally by a happy blending of the indigenous and Islamic modes of construction and ornamentation. With the exception of Humāyūn's tomb (pp. 38, 107), which does not appear to have been built personally by him, no distinct Mug͟hal style had taken form yet. Akbar, however, gave it a character of its own for the first time.

Akbar's seat of government was, however, not Delhi but Agra, where he built his famous fort, and not much far raised the new town of Fatehpur Sikri. His tomb at Sikandara also lies on the outskirts of Agra. During the early years of his reign, however, certain buildings were also constructed in Delhi, and he may have been interested even personally in some of them. Adham K͟hān, son of Māham Anga, a wet-nurse of Akbar, and one of his generals, killed Ataga K͟hān, a minister and husband of Jī Jī Anga, another wet-nurse. This enraged Akbar, and he had Adham K͟hān thrown down from a terrace. His tomb at Mehrauli, built in 1562, is octagonal and is in the Lodī style, with the difference that it lacks the usual *chhajja* (p. 60). Māham Anga herself built in 1561-62 the K͟hairu'l-Manāzil-Masjid (p. 127) in front of the Purana-Qila. Ataga Khān's tomb, built in 1566-67 in Nizamuddin, is a square chamber within a walled enclosure. Of red sandstone, and with three recessed arches on the sides, it follows the elevation of Humāyūn's tomb on a smaller scale, but is much more ornamented.

(*v*) *Jahāngīr* (*1605-1627*)

After Akbar's death in 1605, his son Salīm by the Amber princess, ascended the throne under the name of Jahāngīr. By nature he was pleasure-loving, and fond of natural beauty. Being well-versed in Persian literature, he was given even to composing poems at times. Miniature painting attracted him most, and, in fact, the development of Mughal painting owes in no small measure to his direct patronage. He had, however, little interest in architecture.

He spent the greater part of his life at Lahore and Kabul, and this may account for his interest in developing communications by laying roads and erecting *kos-mīnārs*, bridges and sarais along them. The tombs of his father and father-in-law are two major monuments at Agra in which he took interest. Towards the later part of his reign certain monuments were also raised in Delhi, but he had no hand in their construction. The Chaunsaṭh-Khambā ('sixty-four pillars') in Nizamuddin with its sixty-four pillars (p. 119), was utilized as a tomb for Mīrzā 'Azīz Kokaltāsh, son of Jī Jī Anga and Ataga Khān, after his death in 1623-24. Bairam Khān's son, Mīrzā 'Abdu'r-Raḥīm Khān-i-Khānān, who served both Akbar and Jahāngīr and who was a scholar knowing several languages and wrote couplets in Hindi under the familiar name of Raḥīm, lies buried in a massive tomb close to Nizamuddin (pl.XX B; p.120). Originally faced with red sandstone relieved by the use of buff sandstone and marble, most of which was stripped off for use in Safdar-Jang's tomb (pl. III; p. 89), it is similar to Humāyūn's tomb in basic design.

(*vi*) *Shāh Jahān* (*1628-58*)

Jahāngīr died in 1627, but Shāh Jahān ascended the throne only in 1628, after Dāwar Bakshh, son of Khusraw, Shāh Jahān's elder brother, had ruled for a while and other rivals had been put out of the way. Shāh Jahān inherited the artistic taste of his father, but his interest and enthusiasm went beyond. It was architecture which gripped and gratified him and remained his life-long passion.

By the time he came to the throne, the Mughal empire had at its back almost a continuity of just over a century, during which its artistic traditions had become mature and refined. To these were added his personal interest and patronage, and the result was a remarkable efflorescence of architecture.

Shāh Jahān preferred marble to other stones. His buildings are characterized by a form and feeling of feminity, sensuousness and delicateness, as distinct from the sturdy, robust and relatively plain appearance of the constructions of Akbar. Ornament, therefore, naturally plays a dominant role in his buildings. The chaste and simple relief-work on the red sandstone now gave way to delicate carvings in marble, almost like filigree-work, and to fine inlay and painting. The arch became foliated, and the dome received a Persian form, bulbous in outline and constricted at the neck. The pillars were raised with shafts resting on foliated bases and crowned by involuted bracket-capitals.

Shāh Jahān replanned the forts at Lahore and Agra and added several buildings within them. At Agra, he even demolished some buildings of sandstone and replaced them by marble ones. His highest achievement, however, is the Tāj-Mahal at Agra.

In 1638 he transferred the capital from Agra to Delhi and laid the foundations of Shāhjahānābād, the seventh city of Delhi (p. 142), which is enclosed by a rubble wall, with bastions, gates and wickets at intervals. Of its fourteen gates, some have already been demolished. His famous citadel, the Lal-Qila or the Red Fort (p. 148), at the town's eastern end on the right bank of the Yamuna, was begun in 1639 and completed after nine years. It is different from the Agra Fort, since at its back lies the experience gained by Shāh Jahān at Agra and because it was planned by a single hand. It is an irregular octagon, with two long sides on the east and west, and with two main gates, one on the west and the other on the south, called Lahori (pl. XXII) and Delhi gates respectively. The royal apartments in it, reflecting the life and customs of the contemporary courts in Muslim countries, are concentrated along the eastern river-front while within were originally sited apartments for the emperor's noblemen, relatives and retinue. While the walls, gates and a few other structures in the fort are constructed of red sandstone, marble has been used largely in the palaces.

Within the fort, the entrance to the palace area lies through the double-storeyed Naubat- or Naqqār-Khāna ('drum-house'), where ceremonial music was played, and which also served as the entrance to the court in front of the Dīwān-i-'Ām ('hall of public audience'). Within the latter, a red sandstone rectangular hall (pl. XXIII; p. 150), stood the royal throne under a marble canopy, with an inlaid marble dais below it for the prime minister. The wall behind the throne is ornamented with beautiful panels of *pietra dura* inlay, said to have been executed by Austin de Bordeaux, a Florentine artist.

Originally there were six marble palaces along the eastern water-front. Behind the Dīwān-i-'Ām, but separated by a court, is the Rang-Mahal ('palace of colour'), so called owing to coloured decoration on its interior. It consisted of a main hall, with vaulted chambers on either end; and a channel, called the Nahr-i-Bihisht ('stream of paradise'), ran down through it, with a central marble basin fitted with an ivory fountain. The Mumtāz-Maḥal, originally an important apartment in the imperial seraglio, now houses the Delhi Fort Archaeological Museum.

The Dīwān-i-Khāṣ ('hall of private audience') is a highly-ornamented pillared hall with a marble dais (pl. II; p. 153), which is said to have supported the famous Peacock Throne, carried away by the Persian invader Nādir Shāh. The Tasbīḥ-Khāna ('chamber for counting beads') consists of three rooms, behind which is the Khwābgāh ('sleeping chamber'). On its northern screen is a representation of the Scales of Justice, which are suspended over a crescent amidst stars and clouds (pl. XXIV). The emperor appeared before his subjects every morning at the octagonal tower, Muthamman-Burj, adjoining the eastern wall of the Khwābgāh. A small balcony, which projects from the tower, was added here in 1808 by Akbar Shāh II, and it was from this balcony that King George V and Queen Mary appeared before the people of Delhi in December 1911.

The floors of the Ḥammām ('bath'), consisting of three main apartments, are inlaid with coloured stones. The baths were provided with hot and cold water and one of the fountains in the easternmost apartment is said to have emitted a spray of rosewater. The Ḥayāt-Bakhsh-Bāgh ('health-bestowing garden'), with its pavilions lying to the north of the Ḥammām, was later considerably altered.

In 1644, Shāh Jahān commenced his great mosque, the Jāmi'-Masjid, the largest mosque in India, and completed it in 1650. Built on a raised plinth, it has three imposing gateways approached by long flights of steps, and its prayer-hall, flanked by a four-storeyed minaret at either end, is covered by three large domes ornamented with alternating stripes of black and white marble

Among other buildings of Shāh Jahān's reign in Delhi, important for their association with the royal family, mention may be made of the tombs of Jahānārā and Raushanārā, his daughters. Raushanārā laid out her garden-tomb in 1650, soon after her father had completed <u>Sh</u>āhjahānābād. Jahānārā's tomb in Nizamuddin was built by herself in 1681 and consists of an unroofed small enclosure, walled with latticed marble-screens with a touching inscription on her grave (p. 117). One of <u>Sh</u>āh Jahān's wives. Fateḥpurī Begam, built in 1650 the famous Fateḥpurī mosque at the western end of Chandni-Chowk on the pattern that had now become conventional (p. 144).

(vii) Aurangzeb (1658-1707)

Aurangzeb imprisoned his father <u>Sh</u>āh Jahān and crowned himself as emperor at Delhi in July 1658 at the <u>Sh</u>ālimār garden, which contains now only some derelict buildings with patches of floral paintings (p. 138). After gaining victory over his other three brothers or doing away with them otherwise, he celebrated a second coronation in June 1659, again at Delhi. The Mug<u>h</u>al empire, however, had by now started disintegrating, owing to his puritanical beliefs, bigoted behaviour and other external factors. With his accession, the cultural and intellectual enterprises suffered still worse, and architecture and fine arts succumbed to a decline and oblivion, from which they were never to emerge during the rule of the Mug<u>h</u>als. This was no doubt due in a substantial measure to the dislike of arts by the emperor himself.

The dispositions of <u>Sh</u>āh Jahān and Aurangzeb form a study in contrast. <u>Sh</u>āh Jaḥān participated in the life of his people, joining them in festivities and prayer;

his Jāmi'-Masjid was used both by him and his subjects. But Aurangzeb led an isolated life, withdrawing his whole self unto him. In the Red Fort at Delhi, he built in 1659-60 the small Motī-Masjid ('pearl mosque') for his private use. At Agra, the Nagīna-Masjid ('gem mosque') is also believed to have been built by him for the same purpose, although some authorities ascribe it to Shāh Jahān. The Motī-Masjid, entirely of marble, follows the conventional pattern. With its white surface relieved by borders and other designs in black marble, it is a dainty masterpiece, although its three domes, originally gilded with copper, are perhaps a little too rounded and interfere with a dignified look. Aurangzeb also made some additions to the forts at Delhi and Agra, such as the barbicans in front of the gateways at the former.

The beautiful Zīnatu'l-Masājid or Ghaṭā-Masjid in Daryaganj was built by Aurangzeb's daughter, Zīnatu'n-Nisā Begam, in about 1711, after her father's death. Much smaller than the Jāmi'-Masjid built by her grandfather, it resembles it superficially, with its red sandstone facing, white marble domes with black marble flutings and tall minarets.

G. Later Mughals (1707-1857)

Aurangzeb died in 1707, and the Mughal empire now disintegrated fast, although the successors of the great Mughals continued reigning over the dismembered dominions till 1857. This period was marked by mutual dissensions, gradual entrenchment of foreign powers and raids by the Persian adventurer Nādir S͟hāh and his successor in Afghanistan, Aḥmad S͟hāh Durrānī. The rulers had neither the resources nor the inclination to erect any major monuments. The only significant exception is provided by the tomb of Mīrzā Muqīm Abu'l Manṣūr K͟hān, entitled Ṣafdar-Jang, who was the viceroy of Oudh under Muḥmmad S͟hāh (1719-48) and later prime minister under Aḥmad S͟hāh (1748-54). The tomb was built in about 1754 by S͟hujā'u'd-Daula, Safdar-Jang's son. It is not only the last example of the pattern which began with Humāyūn's tomb, but also follows the latter in essential features. Enclosed within a large garden, divided into squares on the *chahārbāgh* pattern, with tanks and fountains along the central pathways, the double-storeyed mausoleum stands out in the centre of the enclosure. Its exaggerated ornamentation and lack of proportions, evidenced particularly by its vertical elevation, rob it of the character of a great building, although it has been rightly described as 'the last flicker in the lamp of Mug͟hal architecture at Delhi'.

A building of quite a different type which was built in about 1724 during the rule of the later Mug͟hals is Jantar-Mantar (pl. IV; p. 97). It was built by Maharaja Jai Singh II of Jaipur (1699-1743) and is an astronomical observatory with masonry instruments to read the movements of heavenly bodies.

H. THE MODERN PERIOD

In 1857 Delhi came once again into prominence. From the 11th May to the 17th September of that year, it remained in the hands of the first organized fighters for the country's independence. When British authority was restored, Bahādur Sh̲āh II was deported to Rangoon and thus disappeared the last human vestige of the Mug̲hal rule at Delhi. There are several buildings in Delhi associated with this upheaval. Among these are the Magazine Gates (p. 146) near the Delhi General Post Office, the Flagstaff Tower (p. 134) and the Mutiny Memorial (p. 137). The Flagstaff Tower represents the site where the ladies of the British cantonment gathered with their children and servants on the 11th May 1857, before fleeing to Karnal. The Mutiny Memorial, now christened as Ajitgarh, was built in 1863, originally in memory of the officers and soliders who were killed in subduing the so-called Mutiny.

There are also certain other buildings associated with the early British administrators. One of these buildings is the Metcalfe House (p. 141), built in about 1835 by Sir Thomas Metcalfe of the court of Bahādur Sh̲āh II. A few kilometres to the north is the Coronation Memorial, where took place the *Darbār* of 1911, in which the decision to shift the capital of British India from Calcutta to Delhi was announced. This momentous decision led to the creation of New Delhi, where thousands of buildings, many of them monumental in character, were and are still being built. These, however, fall beyond the purview of this book.

4. QUTB AREA

A. Lāl-Kot

The Tomar Rajputs are believed to have settled first in the Sūraj-Kuṇḍ area (p. 100), and shifted later some 10 km west, where Anangpāl raised the citadel of Lāl-Koṭ, now survived by its thick stone-built ramparts, a panoramic view of which may be obtained from the top or balconies of the Qutb-Minar. Recent excavations have shown that the original citadel of Lāl-Koṭ was oblong on plan, and the high stone walls to its west, which enlarge the original enclosure and are usually regarded as its part, are a later construction. Outside the ramparts ran a moat, now traceable only in some places. The later wall mentioned above is provided with massive towers and pierced by several gates, some with outworks, known as Ghazni, Sohan and Ranjit gates.

The rubble-built walls of the ramparts are 2·5 to 3 m thick with a stone footing on the exterior, over which was raised a thick brick revetment. Later, an elegant and impressive veneer of dressed local quartzite blocks, now extant only over some stretches, was raised in front of the brick-face, and provided with neat-looking semi-circular bastions at irregular intervals.

Ruins of several structures can be traced within the Lāl-Koṭ, but no palaces have been located. Its original temple area is now occupied by the Qutb-Minar and other associated monuments.

The walls of Lāl-Koṭ have been pierced by the Delhi-Qutb, Badarpur-Qutb and Mehrauli-Qutb roads, and the visitor can have a glimpse of them while approaching this area from any of these directions, although they are not so apparent, while coming from Mehrauli.

B. Qila Rai Pithora

Vigraharāja IV, the Chauhān prince of Śākambharī, captured Delhi from the Tomars in the later half of the twelfth century (p. 13) and his grandson Pṛithvīrāja III, popularly known by the name of Rai Pithora, extended the Lāl-Koṭ by throwing up massive ramparts around it. This enlarged city, with the Lāl-Koṭ at its south-western base, is known as Qila Rai Pithora and is the first of the so-called seven cities of Delhi. Quṭbu'd-Dīn captured it in 1192 and made it as his capital. Like Lāl-Koṭ, its ramparts are cut through by the Delhi-Qutb and Badarpur-Qutb roads. The road-pierced ramparts of Qila Rai Pithora can be seen by the visitor on both sides of the road just past Adhchini village, as he approaches them from Delhi side. The extents of ramparts are, however, best viewed from the Qutb-Minar.

The rubble-built ramparts are largely covered by débris, and their entire circuit is not traceable. They are 5 to 6 m in thickness, and as high as 18 m. on some sides, with a wide moat outside them. They were pierced by thirteen gates, according to Tīmūr. Among the gates that still exist are Ḥauẓ-Rani, Barka and Budaun gates, the last of which is mentioned by Ibn-Baṭṭūta and was probably the main entrance to the city.

C. Quwwatu'l-Islām-Masjid

Barring the pre-Sultanate monuments of Kutch District, this is the earliest extant mosque in India and consists of a rectangular court, 43·2 m by 33 m, enclosed by cloisters (pl. VIII), erected with the carved columns and other architectural members of twenty-seven Hindu and Jain temples demolished by Quṭbu'd-Dīn Aibak, as recorded by him in his own inscription on the main eastern entrance. Quṭbu'd-Dīn calls the mosque as Jāmi'-Masjid and states that on the original erection of each of the demolished temples a sum of twenty lacs of coins had been spent. Later it came to be called the Quwwatu'l-Islām ('might of Islam') mosque. The western portion of its courtyard occupies the original site of one of the demolished temples. At the two ends of its eastern cloisters, an intermediate storey was raised to provide compartments for the ladies. An iron pillar from a Vishṇu temple of the fourth century which had been earlier set up here probably by Anangpāl (pp.13, 55), stands in front of the prayer-hall (pl. VII).

The mosque was begun in 1192, immediately after the capture of Delhi by Quṭbu'-d-Dīn, and completed in 1198. Later, a massive stone screen was erected in front of the prayer-hall, consisting of a central arch, 6·7 m wide and 16 m high, with two similar but smaller arches on either side, all ogee-shaped (pl. VII). Except for the apex, where the few stones are laid in the manner of voussoirs, the construction of the arches is corbelled. The screen is beautifully carved with borders of inscriptions and geometrical and arabesque designs, but the hand of craftsmen used to Hindu motifs is clearly perceptible in the naturalistic representation of serpentine tendrils and undulating leaves of its scroll-work and even in the fine characters of the Quranic inscriptions.

The mosque was enlarged by two later rulers. Shamsu'd-Dīn Iltutmish (1211-36), son-in-law and successor of Quṭbu'd-Dīn, doubled the size of the mosque in 1230 by extending its colonnades and prayer-hall outside the original enclosure, with the result that the Qutb-Minar now fell within the mosque-enclosure. The arches of Iltutmish's screen are still principally corbelled, although their arabesque ornamentation with the inscriptions standing out prominently is Saracenic in feeling, as distinct from the mixed decoration of Quṭbu'd-Dīn Aibak's screen. 'Alāu'd-Dīn Khaljī (1296-1316) again extended the mosque substantially by enlarging the enclosure. He provided two gateways on the longer eastern side and one each on the north and south, the last one known as 'Alā-ī-Darwāza (pl. XI A; p. 57) and still extant in entirety. In fact, he doubled the area of the mosque, and also commenced the construction of another *mīnār*, intended to be twice the size of Quṭbu'd-Dīn's *mīnār*, although it remained incomplete (pl. XXV).

D. Qutb-Minar

Quṭbu'd-Dīn Aibak laid the foundation of the now world-famous Qutb-Minar (pl. IX), intended possibly mainly as a tower of victory but also as a *mīnār* attached to the Quwwatu'l-Islām mosque for the use of the *mu'adhdhin* ('crier') to call the people to prayer. Surprisingly, a later Nāgarī inscription on the *mīnār* calls it 'Alāu'd-Dīn's victory-column (*vijaya-stambha*). Quṭbu'd-Dīn had perhaps only succeeded in raising the first storey, the remaining storeys being eventually completed by his successor Iltutmish. From the Nāgarī and Persian inscriptions on the *mīnār*, it appears that it was damaged twice by lightning, in 1326 and 1368. The first damage occurred during Muḥammed Tughluq's reign (1325-51), and was repaired by him apparently in 1332. The second damage was attended by Fīrūz Tughluq (1351-88). Later in 1503, Sikandar Lodī (1489-1517) also carried out some restoration in the upper storeys. Originally the *mīnār* had only four storeys, faced with red and buff sandstone. The uppermost storey which was damaged in 1368 during Fīrūz Tughluq's reign, was replaced by him by two storeys, making free use of marble but leaving the lower portion of the fourth storey built with sandstone in its original condition.

The original three storeys are each laid on a different plan, the lowest with alternate angular and circular flutings, the second with round ones and the third with angular ones only, with the same alignment of flutings, however, being carried through them all. Its projecting balconies with stalactite pendentive type of brackets and inscriptional decorative bands on different storeys heighten its decorative effect (pl. X A). It has a diameter of 14·32 m at the base and about 2·75 m on the top. With a height of 72·5 m and 379 steps, it is the highest stone tower in India and a perfect example of *mīnār* known to exist anywhere.

There exists a tradition that the Qutb-Minar was built by Pṛthvīrāja, the last Chauhān king of Delhi, for enabling his daughter to behold the sacred river Yamuna from its top as part of her daily worship. Its entire architecture, however, bespeaks an Islamic origin, with two of its proto-types in brick still existing at Ghazni, although Hindu craftsmen were certainly employed for its construction, as is evident also from certain Devanāgarī inscriptions on its surface. Sometimes sculptured stones from temples have been found utilised in it.

Originally it was surmounted by a cupola, which fell down during an earthquake and was replaced early in the nineteenth century by a new cupola in the late Mug̱hal style by one Major Smith. It looked, however, so incongruous that it was brought down in 1848, and may now be seen on the lawns to the south-east of the *mīnār*.

E. Iron pillar

In the courtyard of the Quwwatu'l-Islām mosque stands the famous iron pillar which bears a Sanskrit inscription in Gupta script, palaeographically assignable to the fourth century, a date which is also confirmed by the peculiar style of its *āmalaka*-capital. The inscription records that the pillar was set up as a standard (*dhvaja*) of god Vishṇu on the hill known as Vishṇupada, in the memory of a mighty king, named Chandra, who is now regarded as identical with Chandragupta II (375-413) of the imperial Gupta dynasty. A deep hole on the top of the pillar indicates that an additional member, perhaps an image of Garuḍa, was fitted into it to answer to its description as a standard of Vishṇu.

The pillar has been brought here evidently from somewhere, else, as no other relics of the fourth century are found at the site. There is a strong bardic tradition that it was brought here—wherefrom, nobody knows—by Anangpāl, the Tomar king who is credited with the founding of Delhi (p. 13). The base of the pillar is knobby, with small pieces of iron tying it to its foundations, and a lead sheet covers the portion concealed below the present floor-level.

The total length of this slightly tapering shaft is 7·20 m, of which 93 cm is buried below the ground. The metal of the pillar has been found to be almost pure malleable iron. Its portion below the ground shows some signs of rusting, but at a very slow rate. The manufacture of such a massive iron pillar, which has not deteriorated much during sixteen hundred years of its existence, is a standing testimony to the metallurgical skill of ancient Indians.

F. Iltutmis̲h̲'s tomb

The tomb of S̲h̲amsu'd-Dīn Iltutmis̲h̲ (1211-36), son-in-law and successor of Quṭbu'd-Dīn Aibak, lies to the north-west of the Quwwatu'l-Islām mosque. It was built in about 1235 by Iltutmis̲h̲ himself, only five years after the construction of Sultan G̲h̲ārī's tomb (p. 68). Yet it is quite different from the latter and illustrates that phase in the development of Indo-Islamic architecture when the builder had ceased to depend for material on the demolition of temples, although the arches and semi-domes below the squinches were still laid in the indigenous corbelled fashion.

Its tomb-chamber with a cenotaph in its centre, internally nearly 9 m sq. and faced with red sandstone, was certainly intended to be covered with a dome, as is clear from the squinches, which appear for the first time in this building. It is believed that the original dome had fallen and was replaced by Fīrūz Shāh Tughluq (1351-88), but even this did not survive. The interior on the west is occupied by three *miḥrābs*, the central one higher and ornamented with marble, to serve as a place for prayers, while the other sides are pierced by arched entrances. The tomb is plain on the outside, but is profusely carved on the entrances and in the interior with inscriptions in Kufi and Naskh characters and geometrical and arabesque patterns in Saracenic tradition, although several motifs among its carvings are reminiscent of Hindu decoration. To this class belong wheel, bell-and-chain, tassel, lotus and diamond. In view of its lavish ornamentation, Fergusson described it as 'one of the richest examples of Hindu art applied to Muhammadan purposes.'

G. 'Alā'ī-Darwāza

The southern gateway of the Quwwatu'l-Islām mosque, as extended by 'Alāu'd-Dīn Khaljī, is known as the 'Alā-ī-Darwāza (pl. XI A), and among its several inscriptions executed to form an ornamental surface, three mention the date of its erection as 710 A.H. (1311).

It is the first building employing wholly the Islamic principles of acurate construction and geometric ornamentation and also betrays certain Saljuqian characteristics which had influenced the <u>Kh</u>aljī architecture (p. 21). Important among these characteristics are wide and bulging dome with a central knob, pointed horse-shoe-shaped arches and squinches and 'lotus-bud' fringes of the arches.

The celebrated gateway, built of red sandstone, is 17·2 m square with arched openings on all sides, and is surmounted by a wide but shallow dome on an octagonal base achieved through squinches with concentric series of arches. The northern arch is semicircular, while others have a pointed horseshoe shape, with radiating voussoirs laid on the principle of true arch. The underside of the arches is fringed with 'lotus-bud' embellishment, not merely in the openings, but also in the perforated side-windows. Its excellent proportions, profuse geometrical carvings on the interior, inscriptional bands of white marble in Nas<u>kh</u> characters and other decorative details in red stone (pl. X B) make it a very pleasing structure. It has been rightly described as 'one of the most treasured gems of Islamic architecture.'

H. 'Alā'ī Mīnār

This unfinished *mīnār* north of the Qutb-Minar was commenced by 'Alāu'd-Dīn <u>Kh</u>aljī, but with its extant height of 24·5 m it had hardly reached its first storey when he died leaving it incomplete. 'Alāu'd-Dīn had doubled the size of the Quwwatu'l-Islām-Masjid, and his *mīnār* was also conceived to be double the height of the Qutb-Minar to be proportionate with the enlarged mosque.

I. 'ALĀU'D-DĪN'S TOMB AND COLLEGE

To the south-west of the Quwwatu'l-Islām mosque lie some rooms and halls in ruins making an L-shaped block. They are believed to represent 'Alāu'd-Dīn's tomb and college (*madrasa*), which was started by him to impart instructions in Islamic theology and scriptures. The central room in the southern wing was perhaps his tomb. The conception of a combined college and tomb appears here in India for the first time and is perhaps inspired by Suljuqian traditions.

J. OTHER MONUMENTS

The gateway through which the visitor enters the Qutb area is, in fact, the entrance to a sarai of the late Mughal period. To the south-east of the 'Alā'ī-Darwāza and approached through its eastern gateway is the small attractive tomb of saint Imām Muhammad 'Alī, better known as Imām Ẓāmin, who was a native of Turkestan and came to India during the reign of Sikandar Lodī (1488-1517). Surmounted by a dome of sandstone covered with plaster and rising from an octagonal drum, its sides are covered with perforated screens, characteristic of the Lodī period. Apparently Imām Zāmin discharged some important duties in connection with the

Quwwatu'l-Islām mosque. He built his tomb according to an inscription in 944 A.H. (1537-38) and died a year later.

About 150 m south-east of the Qutb-Minar is the octagonal tomb of Muḥmmad Qulī Khān, brother of Adham Khān, a general and foster-brother of Akbar (p. 40). Built early in the seventeenth century this tomb was used as his residence during the rains by Sir Charles Theophilus Metcalfe, Resident at the Muhgal court. In fact, he also erected certain other structures for his use in a pseudo-Mughal style, which may still be seen in ruins in the neighbourhood. Two of his stepped pyramidal towers, known as Gaṛhgaj, lie at the rear of the Rest-house and the Canteen.

Within the original Lāl-Koṭ and approached from the Qutb-Mehrauli road is the Jogamāyā temple, built over a century ago during the reign of Akbar II (1806-37), at the site reputed to be that of an ancient temple of the *yoginīs* ('female semi-divine beings'), from which Delhi derived the alternate name of Yoginīpura (p. 16). To its north, outside the original Lāl-Koṭ is a tank in ruins, called Anang-Tāl, which is said to have been built by Anangpāl.

5. MEHRAULI

A. Adham Khān's tomb

Adham Khān's tomb lies to the north of the Qutb-Mehrauli road immediately before one reaches the town

Lying on the walls of Lāl-Koṭ and rising from a terrace enclosed by an octagonal wall provided with low towers at the corners, it consists of a domed octagonal chamber in the Lodī style, with a verandah on each side pierced by three openings, without however, the usual *chhajja* (eaves) below the parapets. It is known popularly as Bhūl-Bhulaiyān ('labyrinth'), for a visitor often loses his way amidst the several passages in the thickness of its walls.

Adham Khān, son of Māham Anga, a wet nurse of Akbar, was a nobleman and general in Akbar's army. In 1562 he fell out with Ataga Khān, husband of Jī Jī Anga, another wet nurse, and killed him, whereupon he was thrown down from the ramparts of Agra Fort by the order of the emperor and died. His mother also soon passed away out of grief, and both were buried in this tomb built by Akbar.

B. Bāolīs (stepped wells)

There are several stepped wells (*bāolīs*) built with rubble stone in and around Mehrauli, two among which are better known than others. Gandhak-kī-Bāolī, so called because of the smell of sulphur (*gandhak*) in its waters, lies about 100 m south of Adham Khān's tomb. Believed to have been built in the reign of Iltutmish (1211-36), it has five tiers, with a circular well at its southern end. It is also known as the diving well, since divers jump into it from the upper tiers for the amusement of visitors.

Further 400 m south is another four-tiered stepped well, known as Rājon-kī-Bain, which seems to have derived its name from being used by masons (*rāj*). Steps within its top walls connect it with a mosque, wherein a *chhatrī* bears an inscription of 912 A.H. (1506), stating that it was built during the reign of Sikandar Lodī (1489-1517).

C. Dargāh-Quṭb-Ṣāhib

K͟hwāja Quṭbu'd-Dīn Bak͟htyār Kākī, popularly known as Quṭb-Ṣāhib, and surnamed Kākī because during his meditation he was fed on small cakes known as *kāks*, was born at Ush in Persia. He came to India with the earliest Muslim conquerors after journeying through Khurasan and Baghdad and became a disciple, and later a spiritual successor, of K͟hwāja Mu'inu'd-Dīn Chis͟htī of Ajmer. He lived during the reign of Iltutmis͟h (1211-1236) and died in 1236.

His grave, originally plain and earthen, but now enclosed within marble balustrades and surmounted by a dome resting on pillars, completed as late as 1944, is the main shrine in the *dargāh*. It lies in the middle of a rectangular enclosure, which has been embellished by different rulers of Delhi, the most pleasing part being the western wall containing floral multi-coloured tiles, said to have been fixed by Aurangzeb.

The saint was held in high esteem by different rulers, and several of them lie buried in the various enclosures around his grave, the whole place being turned into a kind of necropolis. Among those buried here are Bahādur S͟hāh I (1707-12), S͟hāh 'Ālam II (1759-1806), Akbar II (1806-37) and members of their families. Bahādur Shāh II (1837-57) prepared a grave here for his burial, but it remained unutilized, as he was deported to Rangoon where he died and was buried.

The *dargāh* is provided with several gates, halls for different purposes, such as the Naubat-Khāna ('drum-house'), Majlis-Khāna ('assembly-house') and Tosh-Khāna ('robe-chamber'), mosques, tanks and a *bāolī*. According to an inscription on its main northern gate, it was erected in 1542, during Sher Shāh's reign (1538-1545) by Shaikh Khalīl, a descendant of saint Farīdu'd-Dīn Shakarganj, who was himself a disciple and successor of Khwāja Quṭbu'd-Dīn Kākī. Among important mosques is the small marble-built Motī-Masjid ('pearl mosque'), with three arched openings, and double-storyed *mīnārs* at the eastern corners of its courtyard. It is believed to have been built about 1709 by Bahādur Shāh I. Farrukhsiyar (1713-19) added two gates to the enclosure of the *dargāh*.

Outside the western entrance of the *dargāh*, known as the Ajmeri gate, are the ruins of Ẓafar-Maḥal, a palace built by Akbar II, the main gateway of which is said to have been reconstructed by Bahādur Shāh II and named after his *nom de plume* Ẓafar. Built of red sandstone relieved by marble, it is a lofty, three-storeyed imposing structure, with arcades inside it flanked by rooms on the same pattern as in the Chhatta-Chowk in the Red Fort (p. 149).

D. Ḥauẓ-i-Shamsī

On the southern outskirts of Mehrauli is this large

tank (*Ḥauẓ*) said to have been built about 1230 by S͟hamsu'd-Dīn Iltutmis͟h (1211-36). The tradition is that the Prophet appeared once to Iltutmis͟h in a dream and pointed out this site to him as suitable for building the tank which he had in mind. The next morning Iltutmis͟h noticed here the print of one of the hoofs of the Prophet's horse, around which he built a domed platform and excavated the tank.

The famous Moorish traveller Ibn-Baṭūa was struck by the vastness of this tank, which was supplied by rain water and in the centre of which stood a double-storeyed stone pavilion, reached only by boats when full. A red sandstone domed pavilion resting on twelve pillars located near the south-western corner of the tank, but originally believed to have been situated in its centre, is identified with the pavilion built by Iltutmis͟h. The original stone with hoofprint is believed to have been removed, the present stone being a later renewal.

The waters of the tank are regarded as sacred, and several graves of Muslim saints lie around it. The procession for the fair called Phūlwālon-kī-Sair or Sair-i-Gulfaros͟hān, when flower-vendors present flower-bedecked large fans at the *dargāh* of Quṭb-Ṣāhib and at the Jogamāyā temple, starts from the overflow outlet of this tank, called Jharna.

E. Jahāz-Maḥal

Consisting of a rectangular courtyard in the centre and arched chambers on the sides, with an entrance from the east, this building, located on the north-east corner of Ḥauz-i-S̲h̲amsī, was built perhaps during the Lodī period (1451-1526) and may have served as a pleasure-resort or pilgrims' apartments (pl. XX A). A *miḥrāb* in its western wall suggests that part of it was intended as a mosque for private use. There are several designs of squinches in its chambers. Its corners are surmounted by square *chhatrīs*, and the gateway by a domed pavilion ornamented with blue tiles. At present, the main function of Phūlwālon-kī-Ṣair is held here. It may have acquired the name of Jahāz-Maḥal, from its appearance like a *jahāz* (ship) by the side of a vast lake.

6. MEHRAULI BYPASS

A. BALBAN'S TOMB

On the western side of the Mehrauli bypass to Gurgaon there are extensive ruins of old Mehrauli, now deserted. Among these, as the visitor proceeds from the Qutb-Minar, he first encounters a domeless and extremely dilapidated rubble-built square chamber with arched openings in all its four sides, believed to be G̲h̲iyāthu'd-Dīn Balban's tomb. It occupies an important place in the development of Indo-Islamic architecture, as we find here for the first time the use of a true arch.

A ruined rectangular chamber on its east is believed to have contained the grave of Balban's son, Muhammad, who was popularly known as K̲h̲ān S̲h̲ahīd (i.e., the K̲h̲ān who became a martyr), after he died fighting in a battle against the Mongols near Multan in 1285. There exists also another tomb not very far away to the south, which is also popularly known as that of Khān Shahīd.

B. Jamālī-Kamālī's mosque and tomb

Jamālī was the *nom de plume* of Shaikh Fazlu'llah, also known as Jalāl Khān, a saint and poet who lived from Sikandar Lodī's reign to that of Humāyūn. The mosque associated with his name lies about 300 m south of Balban's tomb and was commenced in about 1528-29 during Bābur's reign and completed during that of Humāyūn. His tomb, lying adjacently, was built also perhaps in about 1528-29, before his death in 1535-36. Since there are two graves in the tomb, one believed to be that of Jamālī, and the other that of Kamālī, an unknown person, the monuments go under a 'double-barrelled' name.

The original gate to the mosque, still surviving, lies on the south. Its prayer-hall is pierced by five arches, inclining towards a four-centred form and ornamented with carved bands and medallions in the spandrels. The central arch, higher than the others, is more profusely decorated and flanked by fluted pilasters. The niches in the western wall are also decorated, the central and northern ones with Quranic inscriptions. Two staircases at either end of the prayer-hall lead to a narrow gallery running right round the mosque on the second storey with three oriel windows at the rear, one on the south and a small window above the central arch. The rear corners are occupied by octagonal towers. Below the parapet in front are pendant lotus-buds. A single dome covers the central bay.

Architecturally this elegant mosque marks the transition from the Moṭh-Masjid (p. 78) to S͟her S͟hāh's mosque (p. 126), with both of which it shares certain features.

The tomb of Jamālī-Kamālī lies immediately to the north of the mosque within an enclosure. Its small chamber is flat-roofed, and its ceiling and walls are highly ornamented with coloured tiles and patterns in incised and painted plaster, including inscribed verses composed by Jamālī.

C. Māḍhī-Masjid

Among several other mosques in the neighbourhood, a mosque popularly known as Māḍhī-Masjid and situated about 500 m south of the Jamālī-Kamālī-Masjid is somewhat unusual. Its prayer-hall combines the features of an open wall-mosque and a covered mosque. On either side of its three central bays on the wall-mosque are flat-roofed chambers with arched openings. It is profusely ornamented with coloured tiles.

Its domed square gateway on the east is built with grey stone, with projecting windows of red stone. With its comparatively massive proportions, recalling the gateway of the Baṛa-Gumbad mosque (p. 92) of the Lodī period, it is very impressive from the roadside. It is likely to have been built in the Lodī or early Mug͟hal times.

7. SULTAN GHĀRĪ'S TOMB

About 8 km south-west of the Qutb-Minar, on the Mehrauli-Palam road, is Sultan Ghārī's tomb, the first example of a monumental Muslim tomb in India excepting some pre-Sultanate monuments in Kutch District. From an inscription on its main gateway, we learn that it was built in 1231 by Iltutmish (1211-36) over the remains of his eldest son and heir-apparent, prince Nāṣiru'd-Dīn Maḥmūd. The prince had waged several wars on his father's behalf and had died in 1229 at Lakhnauti. The monument exemplifies the same phase in tomb-architecture, as we find in the Quwwatu'l-Islām mosque: it is built with architectural members removed from temples and employs the trabeate construction with which the indigenous architects were familiar.

Around an octagonal tomb-chamber resting on two-tiered pillars removed from earlier temples was raised here a square platform to about half the height of the chamber by piling up rubble stones, so that approached from the platform, now serving the purpose of a courtyard, the chamber assumed the character of a crypt (*ghār*). The chamber was roofed by providing beams and lintels and covered with lime-concrete (pl. XIII). A recently-discovered flight of steps in the core of the wall, connected with the opening on the south, suggests that the original approach to the interior was perhaps through this staircase, the opening through the veneer having been pierced later. The high platform is enclosed by colonnades on the east and west and plain walls on the other two sides, with domed bastions on the corners, which give the monument the appearance of a small fortress. The corridors probably served as a *madrasa* or college. In the centre of the western wing is a prayer-niche of marble, raised on pillars and provided with a *miḥrāb* richly ornamented with Quranic inscriptions. A marble *yoni-paṭṭa* (base slab for a *liṅga*) is found re-used in the floor of this prayer-chamber. The exterior of the tomb-chamber is faced with marble stones over an earlier grey sandstone veneer, and appears to have been the work of Fīrūz Shāh (1351-88), who mentions having carried out certain repairs here.

Recently some sculptured lintels (pl. V A) and an upright stone of a railing from some temple have been discovered embedded in the thickness of the roof concrete, suggesting that a temple existed here in about the seventh-eighth century. They re-used grey stone and marble in several places, as well as the *āmalakas* lying here, appear to come from a different and later temple (p. 12).

To the south of Sultan Ghārī's tomb lie the pillared tombs of Ruknu'd-Dīn Fīrūz Shāh (died 1237) and Mu'izzu'd-Dīn Bahrām Shāh (died 1241), sons of Iltutmish, who occupied the throne subsequently for brief periods, the former in 1235 and the latter in 1241.

A Sanskrit inscription dated in 1361 on a slab found used in a house of later date to the west of the tomb records the digging of a tank on the occasion of a marriage-ceremony, while a stone *linga* is found used as a lintel in a blind arch. A mosque in ruins in the neighbourhood was possibly built by Fīrūz Shāh, while other remains here may belong to the late Mughal period.

8. MAHIPALPUR

The village of Mahipalpur, by tradition associated with an otherwise unknown Tomar king Mahīpāl, lies 4 km west of Sultan Ghārī's tomb on the Mehrauli-Palam road. Immediately to the south-west of the village is a large bund of rubble-masonry, believed to have been constructed by Fīrūz Shāh Tughluq as part of his irrigation-schemes.

Within the village lies a two-aisle deep stone-built hall, with three arched openings, with a room at either end. Its roof is enclosed within stone railings, characteristic of Fīrūz Shāh's architecture (p. 25). Now used as a school, and commonly known as the Maḥal ('palace'), it was possibly built as a hunting lodge by Fīrūz Shāh, to hunt the wild animals coming to the bund for water.

9. PALAM MOSQUE

At the south-east corner of the village of Palam, which is known for its Sanskrit inscription (p. 15) and which was visited by Ibn-Baṭṭūta, exists a small brick-built mosque, with three arched openings in its prayer-hall, and with small domed minarets on the four corners of its roof. According to an inscription in mixed Arabic and Persian prose on the northern arch of its central compartment, it was built by one Ghaẓanfār in 935 A.H. (1528 29) in the reign of Bābur (1526-30); it is thus the only surviving building of Bābur's reign in Delhi and one of the few of his period in India (p. 34). A second inscription in Persian verse on the mosque repeats the same subject-matter with some minor variation.

10. BEGAMPUR

A. Begampurī-Masjid

A narrow road by the side of Aurobindo Ashram (Delhi Branch), 15 km from Delhi on the Delhi-Mehrauli Road, now known as Sri Aurobindo Road, leads to the village of Begampur. Within the village is the Begampurī-Masjid, one of the seven mosques reputed to have been built by Khān-i-Jahān Jūnān Shāh, Fīrūz Shāh Tughluq's prime minister (p. 27).

With a large courtyard, 94 m by 88 m, enclosed by arched cloisters on the sides and a three-aisle deep prayer-hall, the rubble-built structure of the mosque rises from a high plinth. Its corridors are pierced with gates on the north, south and east, with rows of windows on their either side, the last named gate functioning as the main entrance. The façade of the prayer-hall is broken by twenty-four arched openings, the central one being the highest and flanked by tapering minarets in the Tughluq style (pl. XIX A). The central compartment of the prayer-hall is surmounted by a large dome, while small low domes, characteristic of the Tughluq architecture, rise on the roof from the central aisle and from the corridors. At the rear the location of the *miḥrābs* in the interior is indicated by five projections.

B. Bijai-Mandal

Not far from the Begampurī-Masjid to its north lies Bijai-Manḍal, an unusual rubble-built massive octagonal structure on a high platform, with sloping sides in the Tughluq fashion and a doorway at each cardinal point. A temporary cover could be fitted on poles at the south-western corner of its roof, while there also existed perhaps an open pavilion. Immediately to its east lie the remains of an arcaded residential building, which apparently formed part of a mansion.

The purpose of the building, is however, not clear. It is regarded as a bastion of Jahānpanāh (p. 73) by some, while it is believed to have been used later as his residence by Shaikh Ḥasan Ṭāhir, a saint of Sikandar Lodī's reign (1489-1517). Muhammad Shāh Tughluq (1325-51) is said to have used it as a tower for reviewing his troops.

C. Kalu-Saraj-Masjid

The small village of Kalu-Sarai lies about 500 m north-west of Bijai-Manḍal, and may be approached either from that direction or direct from the main

Delhi-Mehrauli road, about 15 km from Delhi. A rubble-built but plastered mosque here, originally with seven arched openings in the façade of its prayer-hall, some of which have now collapsed, is surmounted by a series of low domes in the Tug͟hluq style. It is believed to be one of the seven mosques built by K͟hān-i-Jahān Jūnān S͟hāh, prime minister of Fīrūz S͟hāh Tug͟hluq (p. 27).

D. Jahānpanāh

Jahānpanāh is the name of the fourth city of Delhi, built by Muḥammad bin Tug͟hluq (1325-51) by enclosing the then inhabited area between Qila Rai Pithora and Sīrī, the first two cities of Delhi. The stone-built walls of the city have now been removed over long stretches by the needs of the expanding suburban townships of Delhi. The walls cross the Delhi-Mehrauli road about 14·5 km from Delhi, and can be seen at several points, such as to the north of the Indian Institute of Technology, to the north of Begampurī and south of Khiṛkī mosques (pp. 71, 75), to the north of Chiragh-Delhi (p. 77), at Satpula (p. 76), and close to the Hauz-Rani gate of Qila Rai Pithora.

In a small scale excavation carried out in 1964-65 a portion of the walls of Jahānpanāh near its junction with the eastern wall of Qila Rai Pithora was exposed. The excavation revealed three stages of construction and additions, with rough and small stones in the foundations and a neat ashlar face on the exterior in the wall above the ground.

11. MALAVIYANAGAR AREA

A. Shaikh Kalīru'd-Dīn's tomb or Lāl-Gumbad

Immediately before reaching Malaviyanagar by the road forking south-east from Delhi-Mehrauli road, one sees on the south of the road Shaikh Kabīru'd-Dīn Auliya's tomb, also known as Lāl-Gumbad or Rakābwāla-Gumbad. It consists of a square chamber with battered walls faced with red sandstone and the roof surmounted by a plastered conical dome, resembling thus Ghiyāth-u'd-Dīn Tughluq's tomb (p. 102). Its entrance is on the east through a pointed arch, decorated with marble bands. The iron rings (called *rakāb* here) on its western wall are believed to have been fixed for scaling up the walls by thieves, who are said to have removed its golden finial, from which it has acquired its popular name of Rakābwāla Gumbad.

The tomb is believed to have been built in about 1397. Shaikh Kabīru'd-Dīn Auliya, who is buried here, was a disciple of Shaikh Raushan Chirāgh-i-Dihlī, whose tomb is described elsewhere (p. 77).

B. Shaikh 'Alāu'd-Dīn's tomb

Between Malaviyanagar and Chiragh-Delhi, not far from the road lies the square domed tomb of Shaikh 'Alāu'd-Dīn, a descendant of the famous saint Shaikh Farīdu'd-Dīn Shakarganj. He died in 1541-42, although he built his tomb earlier in 913 A.H. (1507), as seen from an inscription over its doorway.

The tomb-chamber rests on twelve columns, the space between them on the outside having been screened by perforated slabs. Its dome rises from a sixteen-sided drum. With incised and coloured plaster-medallions on the spandrels of arches, merlon designs on the parapets similarly treated, and inscriptional bands on the ceiling of the dome, considerable decorative effect has been achieved in this tomb.

C. Shaikh Yūsuf Qattāl's tomb

A road along the eastern periphery of Malaviyanagar leads to the village Khiṛkī to its south. About 300 m north-west of the village is the small but attractive tomb of Shaikh Yūsuf Qattāl, a disciple of Qāẓī Jalālu'd-Dīn of Lahore. He died in about 1527, after which the tomb was built. Like Shaikh 'Alāu'd-Dīn's tomb, described above, this tomb also rests on twelve pillars, with other details also being similar. Close by are the remains of a mosque and several graves.

D. Khiṛkī-Masjid

This mosque lies on the southern periphery of the village Khirki. Built with rubble stone, and thickly plastered, it is double-storyed, the lower storey consisting only of a series of basement cells. Battered bastions occupy its four corners, imparting it the look of a fortified building. Gateways project from its three sides, except on the west, each flanked by tapering minarets, the main entrance being from the east (pl. XV).

Corresponding with the openings of cells on the lower storey, the upper storey contains perforated windows (*khirkīs*), which have given it its present name. The pillared courtyard is divided into twenty-five squares, five on each side, each square consisting of nine smaller squares. Among the larger squares, three on each side, two on the corners and one in the middle, together with the square in the centre of the courtyard, are each covered with a cluster of nine small low domes of Tughluq pattern. Among the remaining squares, four on the diagonals are left uncovered to admit light, while the others are covered with flat roofs. This ingenious way of covering the courtyard is repeated only in one other mosque erected by the same builder (p.118). These two are the only examples of closed mosques in northern India.

The mosque was built by K̲h̲ān-i-Jahān Jūnān S̲h̲āh, prime minister of Fīrūz S̲h̲āh Tug̲h̲luq (1351-88), and is believed to be one of the seven mosques built by him.

E. SATPULA

Lying about 800 m east of the Khirkī-Masjid and forming part of the enclosure-wall of Jahānpanāh (p. 73), Satpula is a weir, built by Muhammad S̲h̲āh Tug̲h̲luq (1325-51), to regulate the impounded waters for purposes of irrigation.

It is an unique structure, with eleven openings, two at each end being of a subsidiary nature, and the remaining ones giving it its present name (meaning 'seven bridges', or 'bridge with seven openings'). The sides of the openings are provided with grooves for sliding the shutters. At each end is a tower, with an octagonal chamber within, once utilized for a school, from which the monument derives its alternate name of *madrasa.*

12. CHIRAGH-DELHI

A. Chirāgh-i-Dihlī's dargāh

The village of Chiragh-Delhi, on Malaviyanagar-Kalkaji road, grew up slowly around the tomb of Nāṣiru'd-Dīn Maḥmūd entitled Raushan Chirāgh-i-Dihlī ('illuminated lamp of Delhi'), disciple of Ḥaẓrat Niẓāmu'd-Dīn whom he also succeeded as head of the Chishtī sect. He died in 1356. The village was enclosed earlier within a large rubble-built rectangular enclosure with a gateway on each side, by Muḥammad bin Tughluq (1325-51).

The tomb consists of a twelve-pillared square chamber, enclosed within perforated screens and surmounted by a plastered dome rising from an octagonal drum, with small domed turrets at the four corners. It has been renovated, decorated and provided with several halls from time to time, such as a Majlis-Khāna ('assembly hall'), Mahfil-Khāna ('symposium hall') and several mosques among which one was built by king Farrukhsiyar (1713-19). There exist also numerous tombs and graves inside the enclosure of the *dargāh.*

B. Buhlūl Lodī's tomb

The tomb of Buhlūl Lodī (1451-88), founder of the Lodī dynasty, consists of a square chamber, with three arched openings on each side and surmounted by five domes, the central one being larger than the others. The arches are decorated with Quranic inscriptions and medallions in their spandrels. Compared with the tombs of most other rulers of Delhi, it is a plain structure.

13. MOTH-MASJID

Moth-Masjid or Moṭh-kī-Masjid, also the name of the village in which it is located, can be reached either from the Delhi-Mehrauli road by the side of Yusuf-Sarai or from the Ring Road through the colony called New Delhi South Extension II. It was built by Miyān Bhuwa, a minister of Sikandar Lodī (1488-1517), who also served Ibrāhīm Lodī (1517-26) before he earned his wrath and was killed by him.

The mosque rises from a raised platform enclosed by walls, with an elegant red sandstone gate on the east. Its prayer-chamber, veneered with grey ashlar stone, is pierced by five arched openings, the central one being built with red sandstone, and ornamented with marble, with a small window above the arch. The central *miḥrāb* in the prayer-chamber is ornamented with Quranic inscriptions in Naskh characters and the ceilings of the end-bays with incised plaster.

PLATE I

Humāyūn's tomb. *See p. 107*

PLATE II

PLATE III

Safdar-Jang's tomb. *See p.* 89

PLATE IV

Jantar Mantar: Samrāṭ-yantra with Jai Prakāsh and Rām Yantras in background. See p. 97

A. *Frieze from Sultan Ghārī's tomb. See pp. 11 and 69*

B. *Vishṇu from the Qutb area. See p. 14*

PLATE VI

PLATE VII

Quwwatu'l-Islām-Masjid : prayer-hall screen with the iron-pillar. *See p. 52*

PLATE VIII

Quwwatu'l-Islām-Masjid : colonnade of temple-pillars. *See p. 52*

PLATE IX

Qutb-Minar. See p. 53

PLATE X

B. 'Alā'ī-Darwāza : details of decorated façade.

... other ornamentation

A. *'Alā'ī-Darwāza : entrance.* *See p. 57*

B. *'Īsā-Khān's tomb.* *See p. 111*

PLATE XII

A. *Tughluqabad : ramparts and bastions.* *See p. 102*

B. *Tughluqabad : G̲h̲iyāt̲h̲u'd-Dīn's tomb.* *See p. 103*

PLATE XIII

Sultan Ghārī's tomb : mortuary-chamber with colonnade of temple-pillars in background. *See p. 68*

PLATE XIV

A. *Kotla Firoz Shah : pyramidal structure with Aśokan pillar.* *See p. 1*

B. *Hauz-Khas : double-storeyed colonnade of the madrasa.* *See p. 81*

PLATE XV

Khiṛki-Masjid : entrance. *See p. 75*

PLATE XVI

A. *Bāgh-i-'Ālam-kā-Gumbad.* *See p. 81*

B. *Sikandar Lodī's tomb.* *See p. 94*

PLATE XVII

Baṛā-Gumbad : tomb and mosque. *See p. 92*

PLATE XVIII

A. *Qal'a-i-Kuhna-Masjid : façade of prayer-hall.* *See p. 126*

B. *Jāmi'-Masjid : façade of prayer-hall.* *See p. 146*

A. *Begampurī-Masjid : façade of prayer-hall.* *See p. 71*

B. *Moṭh-Masjid.* *See p. 79*

PLATE XX

A. *Jahāz-Maḥal.* *See p. 65*

B. *Khān-ī-Khānān's tomb : southern façade.* *See p. 120*

Purana-Qila : excavated site. *See p. 124*

PLATE XXII

The roof is crowned by three domes, rising from the centre-and end-bays. At the rear-corners are double-storeyed towers with arched openings (pl. XIX B), and to match with them the eastern corners of the compound wall are provided with domed octagonal *chhatrīs*. Other features of the building that draw attention are stalactite pendentives supporting the dome and coloured tile-work, which exists now only in traces.

Built before the Jamālī-Kamālī-Masjid (p. 66), this mosque occupies a significant position in the evolution of the Mug̱ẖal mosque (p. 31). Ornamentation of the *miḥrāb* and arches, special treatment of the central arch and construction of three domes over the prayer-chamber are some of its features found in the Mug̱ẖal mosques, while there are other characteristics which it shares with the Jamālī-Kamālī-Masjid and S̲ẖer S̲ẖāh's mosque (p. 126).

It is said that Sikandar once picked up a grain of *moṭh* (a kind of lentil) from a mosque and handed it over to his minister Miyān Bhuwa, who sowed it and multiplied the grain, and kept on multiplying the proceeds again and again till they earned sufficient money to built this mosque, which has given it its present name.

14. HAUZ-KHAS

A road branching off the Delhi-Mehrauli road (named now Sri Aurobindo Road) south of the Green Park, terminates at Hauz-Khas (Ḥauẕ-Ḵẖāṣ).

'Alāu'd-Dīn Khaljī (1296-1316) excavated a large tank here for the use of the inhabitants of Sīrī, the second city of Delhi founded by him (p. 83). It was then known as Ḥauẓ-i-'Alā'ī. Fīrūz Shāh Tughluq (1351-88) desilted it and put it in repairs, and built several buildings on its southern and eastern banks, which are now known as Hauz-Khas, and are enclosed partly within modern walls.

Fīrūz Shāh's tomb, a rubble-built but plastered square chamber with high but slightly battered walls and a lofty dome, is the most prominent among these buildings. The monotonous austere look of its exterior is broken by a string-course of red sandstone and marble and by carved battlements. The tomb is entered through a door on the south, with a courtyard enclosed within stone railings outside it. The intrados and ceiling of the dome and squinch-pendentives are decorated with plaster-work, including incised Quranic inscriptions in Naskh characters and painting. The inscription over the southern doorway was incised in 913 A.H. (1507) during Sikandar Lodī's reign, when he undertook some repairs to the tomb. The doorway spanned by a lintel and the stone-railings outside it are features of early Indian construction, which have been pleasantly mingled with characteristics of Islamic architecture. Among the four graves inside the chamber, the central one is believed to be that of Fīrūz Shāh and two others of his son and grandson.

Contiguous with the tomb to its west and north rise from the bank of the tank in two storeys a series of halls and chambers, which were built by Fīrūz Shāh n about 1352 as a *madrasa* or college for religious training (pl. XIV B). At their northern extremity is a mosque. These buildings are sited on an L-shaped plan. With heir latticed windows, medallions in stucco, lotus-notif, paintings on ceilings, balconied windows and leep niches, possibly for keeping books, these wings stand out as an unique complex in their class. The independent building on the south-western corner could have served possibly as the principal's residence.

One of the old entrances to the area is from the west, now closed. There are several staircases leading down to the tank from the upper storeys of the *madrasa*. Disposed all over the area, including the neighbourhood of the tank, are several tombs of different designs, but the persons buried in them are not known, although some of these could be the teachers of the college.

In 1398, after defeating Maḥmūd Tug͟hluq, Tīmūr Lane encamped at the tank and his historian S͟harfu'd-Dīn Yāzdī was highly impressed by its large size. He, however, wrongly ascribed the construction of the tank of Fīrūz S͟hāh Tug͟hluq.

15. GREEN PARK AREA

A. BĀG͟H-I-'ĀLAM-KĀ-GUMBAD

Lying between Hauz-Khas and Green Park on he north of the road leading to Hauz-Khas, it is a square structure (pl.XVI A) built with grey ashlar stone and follows the pattern of square Lodī tombs, with semblance of three 'storeys' on the façades (p. 29). There are arched openings on the east, north and south, the last one forming the main entrance, and a *miḥrāb* on the interior on the western side. Its ceiling bears painted incised plaster. According to an inscription on its western wall, it was built in 906 A.H. (1501), during Sikandar Lodī's reign, by one Sultan 'Ābu Sayeed over the grave of Miyān Shaikh Shihābu'd-Dīn Tāj Khān, possibly a saint.

B. Dādī-Potī and other tombs

As one takes the road to Hauz-Khas, from its junction with the Delhi-Mehrauli road, one notices on the north two tombs on an elevated ground, one larger and the other smaller. The tombs, built of rubble and plastered, follow the square pattern of Lodī tombs, with openings on the east, north and south and with the façades broken into semblance of 'storeys'. It is not known who lie buried in them. But the larger one is known as the tomb of Bīwī ('mistress') or Dādī ('grand-mother'), and the smaller one that of Bāndī ('maid-servant'), or Potī ('grand-daughter').

A medieval Sanskrit inscription, much obliterated was recovered here some years back, and the site may represent the location of some Hindu establishment.

There are several other tombs of different size within the Green Park and its neighbourhood, with popular names like Bīran-kā-Gumbad ('brother's dome')

Chhoṭī Gumṭī ('small dome'), Sakrī Gumṭī ('narrow dome') etc., but there is no indication of the persons lying buried in them.

16. HAUZ-KHAS ENCLAVE

A. Sīrī

From the southern tip of Hauz-Khas Enclave, about 13 km from Delhi or from Panch Sheel Road, a road leads east to Sīrī, the second city of Delhi, built by 'Alāud'-Dīn Khaljī in about 1303. The eastern portion of Sīrī is cut across by the wide road connecting Moolchand Hospital and Chiragh-Delhi. Its rubble-built high city-wall is roughly oval on plan. It has survived only in stretches, mostly on the west and south, with remains of some bastions, loopholes for arrows and 'flame'-shaped battlements, which appear to have been introduced here for the first time. Over other portions the alignment of the city-wall is marked by earth and débris. It is said to have possessed seven gates, one of which, towards the south-east, may be seen even now.

No remains of palaces have come to light here. There are, however, some derelict structures in the village of Shahpur-Jat situated inside it on the west. Within or outside the city are, however, the remains of several mosques and tombs, among which the mosque known as Tohfewāla-Gumbad of the Khaljī period, survived only by its domed central compartment, and

Muḥammadwālī and Makhdūm-Ṣāhib's mosques, both of the Lodī period, are well-known.

B. Nīlī-Masjid

Within the Hauz-Khas Enclave lies this rubble-built but plastered mosque, survived now only by its prayer-chamber, pierced by three arched openings and surmounted by a single dome over the central portion. Above the *chhajja*, its façade is ornamented with blue tiles, which have given it its present name, meaning the 'blue mosque'. Over its central archway is an inscription, from which we learn that it was built in 911 A.H. (1505-06) during the reign of Sikandar Lodī (1489-1517), by Kasumbhil, nurse of Fatḥ Khān, son of Khān-i-'Āzam Masnad 'Ālī Khawās Khān, then governor of Delhi.

C. Īdgāh

Not far from the Nīlī-Masjid on its south are the remains of an Idgāh, with a battlemented rubble wall on the west containing a series of eleven *miḥrābs* and originally terminating on the southern and northern ends in a circular bastion, the latter now having disappeared. At the rear are three projections marking the position of the *miḥrābs* on the interior.

An inscription on its southern bastion eulogises Iqbāl Khān, popularly known as Mallū Khān, a powerful noble and virtually the ruler during Maḥmūd Tughluq's reign. It states that the mosque was built by him in 807 A.H. (1404-05), after the devastation wrought by Tīmūr.

D. Chor-Mīnār

About 200 m south-east of the Īdgāh is the Chor-Mīnar, a rubble-built tapering tower, rising from a platform and provided with a staircase in its interior. It was built probably during the Khaljī period.

On its exterior there are several circular holes of unascertained use. It is believed that the heads of thieves (*chor*), who were caught and beheaded, used to be placed in these holes to deter others from engaging in theft, from which it also derives its name.

17. DARYA KHĀN'S TOMB

Close to the market in Kidwai Nagar, approached either from the Delhi-Mehrauli road or from the Ring Road, lie the ruins of a massive tomb, believed to be that of Darya Khān Lohānī, who served all the Lodī kings in several high posts.

With the tomb proper in centre, and domed *chhatrīs* on corners, all built on an extensive three-tiered platform, it is an unique construction. The lowest tier has traces of *chhatrīs* on corners and a gateway and colonnaded chambers in front on the east which make it abundantly clear that originally the entire complex must have presented an impressive and magnificent view. Evidently the tomb occupies the site of an earlier building, some parts of which were exposed during recent excavations.

18. NEW DELHI SOUTH EXTENSION I

There are four noteworthy tombs in this colony, all of the square pattern, and probably built during the Lodī period. Surmounted by a dome, with arched openings on the east, north and south, but with the main entrance from the south, the western wall of their interior is provided with a *miḥrāb*.

About 300 m north of the Ring Road is Kāle K͟hān kā-Gumbad, with its ceiling decorated with painted plaster-work. It has an inscription over the *miḥrāb* in the western wall, from which we learn that it was built in 886 A.H. (1481) during Buhlūl Lodī's reign, to inter the remains of Mubārak K͟hān. There were two nobles of this name at Buhlūl Lodī's court, but the one buried here is likely to be the father of Darya K͟hān, whose tomb, described above, does not lie much far. It is the earliest dated square tomb of the Lodī period and the only one in New Delhi South Extension where we have a clue of the person buried.

At the north end of the colony there are three tombs, collectively known as Tīn-Burj. About 75 m north of the Kāle K͟hān-kā-Gumbad is the so-called Bhūre K͟hān-kā-Gumbad. A short distance to its north again is a little larger Chhoṭe K͟hān-kā-Gumbad. The largest monument to its west is Baṛe K͟hān-kā-Gumbad, 22 m sq. externally. There are domed *chhatrīs* on the four corners of its roof, and the intrados of its dome are ornamented with incised and painted plaster bands, which meet in a decorative medallion in the centre.

19. MUBĀRAK SHĀH'S TOMB

Mubārak Shāh's tomb lies in Kotla-Mubarakpur. Originally it was enclosed by an octagonal compound wall, with two gates on the south and west. But its walls and northern gate have disappeared, leaving only the southern gate and the mosque on the west.

The main entrance to its octagonal chamber is from the south, with arched openings also on the other sides except on the west, which is occupied by a *miḥrāb*. It is surrounded by a verandah, with three openings in each side. The corners are strengthened by sloping buttresses. Its broad low dome rises from a sixteen-sided battlemented drum with a turret on each corner and is crowned by a lantern. Over the roof in the middle of each side stands a *chhatrī*. The ceiling of the dome is ornamented with incised and coloured bands of plaster, with a triple band of Quranic inscriptions at the springing of the dome.

Mubārak Shāh Sayyid, the second ruler of Sayyid dynasty, died in 1434, when the tomb is likely to have been built. With its wide proportions on the ground, low dome, buttresses and *chhatrīs*, the tomb looks a little stunted, but is a good example of octagonal Sayyid tombs, which retained their popularity in the Lodī and even Mughal times (pp. 40, 60).

20. RAMAKRISHNAPURAM AREA

Around the modern colony of Ramakrishnapuram are the villages of Munirka, Muhammadpur, Basantnagar and Kusumpur. This area is dotted with numerous tombs, mosques, pavilions and other structures, some of which are large in size and not entirely devoid of architectural merit, although now somewhat dilapidated. Most of thema ppear to have been built during the Lodī period.

Among the important monuments in the area are the three-domed tomb, called Tīn-Burjī, to the east of the village of Muhammadpur, Malik-Munirka mosque in the village of Munirka, Wazirpur-kā-Gumbad, about one km to its north, the domeless Munḍā-Gumbad within Ramakrishnapuram, another domeless but more massive Munḍā-Gumbad with an octagonal chamber to the south-west of the colony, a little less massive Bāra-Lāo-kā-Gumbad to its east, Bajre-kā-Gumbad, about 500 m north-west of it and another nameless tomb to its north-west bearing an inscription of Sikandar Lodī's reign on its western arch.

21. NAJAF KHĀN'S TOMB

Opposite the Safdarjang Airport (earlier known as Willingdon Aerodrome) on the east of the Delhi-Mehrauli road is Najaf Khān's tomb, with walls of its large garden enclosure and a gateway on the east now in ruins. The mausoleum stands in the centre of the enclosure and consists of a raised platform, originally faced with red sandstone, with two inscribed marble cenotaphs on its top, one belonging to Najaf Khān, and the other to his daughter Fātima. The real graves are in one of the two chambers in the core of the platform. A newly laid garden now covers the enclosure.

Najaf Khān was related to the Safvi kings of Persia and came with his sister to the court of Muḥammad Shāh (1719-48) and later entered the service of Shāh 'Ālam III (1759-1806).He died in 1782 and his daughter earlier in 1820.

22. ṢAFDAR-JANG'S TOMB

The tomb of Mīrzā Muqīm Abu'l Manṣūr Khān, entitled Ṣafdar-Jang (1739-54), viceroy of Oudh under Muḥammad Shāh (1719-48)and later his prime minister is the last example of the garden-tomb layout, which began with Humāyūn's tomb (pl. I; p. 107). It was built in 1167 A.H. (1753-54), according to an inscription over the eastern entrance to the mausoleum, by Nawab Shujā'u'd-Daula, Ṣafdar-Jang's son. Its extensive garden enclosure, over 300 m sq., is divided into four squares by wide pathways and tanks, which are again divided into smaller squares by passages on the pattern of Mughal gardens (*chahārbāgh*). The high rubble walls of the enclosure, with channels over them to carry water to different pavilions, contain series of recessed arches on the interior and octagonal towers (*chhatrīs*) on the four corners. In the centre of the eastern side is the double-storeyed impressive gateway to the enclosure with several apartments, a courtyard and a mosque, while the same position on the other sides is occupied by multi-chambered spacious pavilions, known originally as Moti-

Maḥal ('pearl palace'), Bādshāh-Pasand ('king's favourite'), and Janglī-Maḥal ('sylvan palace'), on the north, south and west respectively. The mosque, built with red sandstone on the second storey, was obviously added later.

The double-storeyed mausoleum, 18·28 m sq. built with red and buffstone relieved by marble, stands in the centre of the garden and rises from a high platform faced by a verandah broken by arched openings, leading to a series of cells on the inside (pl. III). The central chamber of the mausoleum is square with eight apartments around it, the corner apartments being octagonal and the others rectangular. There is one cenotaph in the central chamber, but two graves are located in the underground chamber in the centre of the platform, presumbaly one of Safdar-Jang and the other of his wife. The ceilings of different apartments are ornamented with incised and painted plaster-work. The large dome with its bulbous outline rises from a sixteen-sided drum. The corners of the mausoleum are occupied by polygonal towers picked with inlaid marble designs, and covered by *chhatrīs*. The arched entrances to the tomb-chamber from all the four sides are located within high recessed engrailed arches.

The marble and red sandstone for this building was removed from the tomb of 'Abdu'r Raḥīm Khan Khān-i Khānān (p. 120). With its large garden enclosure, Safdar-Jang's tomb is laid out on the pattern of its prototype, viz., Humāyūn's tomb, but the weakness of its proportions and its pronouncedly vertical elevation, lacking a pyramidal feeling, rob it of a balanced character. With all its weaknesses, the tomb is, however, rightly described as 'the last flicker in the lamp of Mughal architecture at Delhi'.

23. LODI GARDENS

A. Muhammad Shāh's tomb

There exist several monuments of the Sayyid and Lodī periods in the old Lady Willingdon Park, now popularly known as the Lodi Gardens. The tomb of Muḥammad Shāh (1434-44), the third ruler of Sayyid dynasty, follows the typical octagonal pattern, with a central octagonal chamber, surrounded by verandahs, each side pierced by three arched openings, with a running *chhajja* above them. A sloping buttress occupies each angle of the structure. On the roof over the centre of each side is a *chhatrī*, with its dome repeating the outline of the large central dome rising majestically from a sixteen-sided drum, with a turret at each corner. From the drum of the dome rises another series of turrets behind the corner-turrets. The domes are crowned by a sprawling lotus, the other members above them now missing. The ceiling of the dome is decorated.

Each side of the chamber has a beam-and-lintel doorway, although the main entrance is on the south. The openings of the doorways, as also of the outer verandah, were originally closed by perforated screens. The chamber opening on the west was later fully walled, so that it could serve as a mosque. There are eight graves inside, the central one among which is believed to be that of Muhammad Shāh. The general features of this tomb correspond with its precursor, Mubārak Shāh's tomb (p. 87), but with its compactness on plan, high dome and matching *chhatrīs*,—in short, with its better proportions—it is more pleasing.

B. Baṛā-Gumbad-Masjid

About 300 m north-east of Muḥammad Shāh's tomb described above lies the Baṛā-Gumbaḍ (pl. XVII), a square tomb with an imposing dome, turrets on corners and facades possessing a semblance of being double-storeyed. Arches and bracket-and-lintel beams are both used as spans here. On the interior, it is ornamented with stucco work and painting, while on the outside the monotony of grey stone is relieved by the use of red and black stones. The person lying buried in it is not identified, but obviously he must have been an officer of high rank during Sikandar Lodī's reign (1489-1517).

Adjoining the Baṛā-Gumbad on the west is the mosque, known as the Baṛā-Gumbad mosque, which appears to have been erected as an adjunct to the tomb. Built with ashlar stone, the front of its rectangular prayer-hall is faced by five arched openings, the central one sited in a projecting frame. Over the arches runs a *chhajja*. The three central bays of the hall are surmounted by low domes, the end-bays being covered by flat roofs. Oriel windows projecting on its north, south and on the west from the back of the *miḥrāb* bay, are features which distinguish the early Mughal mosques. The rear-corners and the sides of the *miḥrāb*-projection are occupied by tapering minarets in the Tughluq style but seem to anticipate the octagonal towers of the early Mughal and Sūr periods. The mosque is profusely ornamented with coloured tiles and with foliage and Quranic inscriptions wrought in incised and painted plaster. The raised platform in the centre of its courtyard is believed to have contained the grave of its builder, but is more likely to be a small tank for ablution of those offering prayers.

The mosque was built in 900 A.H. (1494) during the reign of Sikandar Lodī (1489-1517), as seen from the inscription over the southern *miḥrāb*. It occupies an important place in the development of the Mughal mosque (p. 31). The dominating position of the Baṛā-Gumbad and the present absence of a grave inside it have misled some scholars to believe that it was raised as a gateway to the mosque. The long hall in front of the prayer-hall appears to have been raised at a later date as a *miḥmān-khāna* or guest house.

C. Shīsh-Gumbad

Shīsh-Gumbad lies about 50 m north of the Baṛā-Gumbad-Masjid. Architecturally it follows the usual pattern of square Lodī tombs with a 'double-storeyed' appearance (p. 28), and is not much different from the Baṛā-Gumbad described above. Its western wall contains a *miḥrāb*, which served as a mosque, but the other sides have a central entrance set in a projecting frame. The *miḥrāb*-projection at the rear and the portion of walls below the string-course are built with alternating narrow and wide courses of stone. Panels of recessed niches run above and below the string-course, the upper ones being pierced by small openings. Inside, the ceiling is decorated with incised plaster-work containing floral patterns and Quranic inscriptions. Originally the tomb was richly decorated with blue tiles, forming friezes below the cornice and the string-course and a border around the horizontal panel above the central entrance on the façades. This decoration, now surviving in traces, gave it its Persian name meaning a 'glazed dome'.

It is not known who lies buried in this tomb, although there exist several graves inside it. It was, however, obviously built during the Lodī period, perhaps during Sikandar Lodī's reign (1489-1517).

D. Sikandar Lodī's tomb

This tomb lies about 250 m north of the Shīsh-Gumbad on the north-western corner of the Lodi Gardens. It is an octagonal tomb, like those of Mubārak Shāh (p. 87) and Muḥammad Shāh, with a central octagonal chamber, surrounded by verandah, with each side pierced by three arches, and the angles occupied by sloping buttresses. The *chhatrīs* over its roof have disappeared (pl. XVI B).

The mausoleum is surrounded by a square garden, enclosed within high walls, with a wall-mosque on the west, and a gateway with outwork on the south, which impart it a dignified setting.

E. Athpula

A little to the east of Sikandar Lodī's tomb lies a bridge with seven arches, their span decreasing from the centre to the bank of the streamlet over which it was built. The word *pula* obviously does not refer to the 'openings', but to piers, of which there are eight (*āṭh*) in this bridge.

Several such bridges were built during the Mughal times, and at least two others are known in and around Delhi (pp. 104 and 121). The Aṭhpula is believed to have been built during Akbar's reign (1556-1605) by one Nawab Bahādur.

24. KUSHK-MAHAL

This monument now lies within the compound of the Tin Murti House,which houses the Nehru Memorial Museum and Library. It is an almost square rubble-built structure, three-aisle deep and with three arched openings resting on stone pillars. Its vaulted ceiling is finished flat on the roof.

It was probably built by Fīrūz Shāh Tughluq (1351-88) and was used by him as one of his several hunting lodges (p. 26). Originally there existed an embankment near it, which stored rain water.

25. SOUTHERN RIDGE

A. Mālcha-Maḥal

Mālcha-Mahal or Mālcha-Bistdarī, approached from Sardar Patel Road about 1 km west of Sardar Patel Crescent (old Willingdon Crescent), is another hunting palace, built by Fīrūz Shāh Tughluq. It is, however, larger than Kushk-Mahal, almost square, with three main bays, the central one larger each bay containing three rooms. Some distance to its south existed a bund which retained rain-water. It has now been converted into a studio for use by artists.

B. Bhūlī Bhatiyārī-kā-Mahal

This monument lies about 500 m south-west of the junction of Panchkuin and Original roads. Like the two preceding monuments, this is also a hunting-palace, built by Fīrūz Shāh Tughluq. Lying on the northern bank of a reservoir enclosed by bunds, only parts of which are now traceable, it consists of a rectangular enclosure, entered through two gateways on its north-eastern corner, and remains of pavilions on the thick southern embankment. The southern and eastern walls of the enclosure are provided with bastions. It is now being used as a Youth Hostel.

According to Sayyid Aḥmad Khān, author of *Āthār-us-Ṣanādīd*, the place was once occupied by a person called Bū'-'Alī Bhaṭṭī, which got corrupted into Bhūlī or Bholī Bhaṭiyārī ('forgetful of simple female innkeeper'), and gave it its present name. The tradition is, however, not backed by evidence.

26. JANTAR-MANTAR

The Jantar-Mantar (pl. IV), an observatory consisting of masonry-built astronomical instruments,lies on the Parliament Street, about 250 m south of Connaught Circus. These instruments were erected by Maharaja Jai Singh II of Jaipur (1699-1743), who was keenly interested in astronomical observations and studied all systems, Western and Eastern, before embarking on his constructions. Initially he built metal instruments, some of which are still preserved in Jaipur, but later discarded them.

The observatory at Delhi was the first to be built, and it was followed by construction of similar observatories at Jaipur, Ujjain, Varanasi and Mathura, the last of which no longer survives. According to tradition Jai Singh built the Delhi observatory in 1710, while Sayyid Aḥmad k͟hān, author of *Āt͟hār-us-Sanādīd*, takes 1724 to be the date of its construction. Since Jai Singh himself mentions that he built the instruments by the order of the emperor (Mḥuammad S͟hāh), who ascended the throne only in 1719 and granted a governorship to him, Sayyid Aḥmad K͟hān's date would appear to be nearer the truth.

Built with brick rubble and plastered with lime,

the instruments have been repaired and restored repeatedly, but without any large scale alteration. Among them, the Samrāṭ-Yantra ('supreme instrument') is 'an equinoctial dial, consisting of a triangular gnomon with the hypotenuse parallel to the earth's axis, and on either side of the gnomon is a quadrant of a circle parallel to the plane of the equator.' The Jai-Prakāsh to its south consists of two concave hemispherical structures to ascertain the position of the Sun and other heavenly bodies. Two circular buildings to the south of the Jai-Prakāsh, with a pillar at the centre, constitute the Rām-Yantra, the walls and floor of which 'are graduated for reading horizontal (azimuth) and vertical (altitude) angles'. The Miśra-Yantra ('mixed instrument') to its north-west combines four instruments in one, and hence its name. These are Niyata-Chakra which indicates the meridian at four places, two in Europe and one each in Japan and the Pacific Ocean; half on an equinoctial dial; Dakshiṇottara-bhitti-Yantra, used for obtaining meridian altitudes and Karka-rāśi-valaya, which indicates the entry of the Sun in the Cancer.

The visitor is advised to consult either of the following books if interested in studying the working of these instruments: (i) *The Astronomical Observatories of Jai Singh*, Calcutta, 1918, and (ii) *A Guide to the old Observatories at Delhi, Jaipur, Ujjain, Benaras*, Calcutta, 1920, both by G. R. Kaye.

To the east of the instruments, the small temple of Bhairava also appears to have been built by Maharaja Jai Singh.

27. HANUMĀN-MANDIR

Situated on the Baba Kharak Singh Road (old Irwin Road) about 250 m south-west of Connaught Circus, this temple is of little architectural importance. The residents of Delhi are, however, particularly devoted to it. The original temple appears to have been constructed by Maharaja Jai Singh about the same time as the Jantar-Mantar, but has undergone large scale renewals since then.

28. UGRASEN-KĪ-BĀOLĪ

A narrow lane off Atul Grove Road (old Hailey Road) cutting across Kasturba Gandhi Road (old Curzon Road) and Sikandra Road, leads the visitor to Ugrasen's Bāolī. Measuring 60 m long north-south and 15 m wide at ground level, and built with rubble and dressed stones it is one of the finest *bāolīs* in Delhi. A long flight of steps flanked by a thick wall with two series of arched niches, the lower ones deep and remaining partly under water, and the upper ones merely recessed from the surface, makes it an impressive sight. There is a circular well at the northern extremity, but between the flight of steps and the well is a covered landing with a terrace or platform at ground level. Between the flanking walls steps lead down to the water level.

Above the flight of steps on the west is a small mosque faced by three openings. With a 'whale-back' roof, but its undersides meeting at an angular apex, four pillared columns of red sandstone carved with *chaitya*-motif and stucco medallions in spandrels, it is an unique structure. The mosque is raised on a solid filling with underground *dālāns* on the sides. Perhaps parts of the entrance complex of the *bāolī* have disappeared. The architectural features of the *bāolī* bespeak a late Tug͟hluq or Lodī age, although traditionally it is said to have been built by Raja Ugrasen, believed to be the progenitor of the Agrawal community. With its deep waters the *bāoli* serves as a swimming pool in summer.

29. SŪRAJ-KUṆḌ

Sūraj-Kuṇḍ lies about 3 km south-east of Tughluqabad in District Gurgaon, and can be reached by a metalled road forking south about 11·5 km from the Qutb-Minar on the Qutb-Badarpur road. The reservoir is believed to have been constructed in the tenth century by king Sūrajpāl of Tomar dynasty, whose existence is based on bardic tradition. The construction consists of a steeped stone embankment on a semi-circular plan to impound the rain-waters from the hills (pl. VI). It is believed that a temple of the Sun existed on its west, certain carved stones from which were recently retrieved from the reservoir, or which are found re-used in later constructions.

Fīrūz S͟hāh Tug͟hluq (1351-88), who took keen interest in irrigation works, had its steps and terraces repaired by laying lime-concrete over them. Later still, a small fortified enclosure, called *gaṛhī*, was raised above the western bank around the traditional site of the temple.

A pool of fresh water oozing from the crevices in the rocks, called Siddha-Kuṇḍ, lies about 600 m south of Sūraj-Kuṇḍ and attracts a large number of pilgrims on certain holy days.

30. ANANGPUR DAM

About 2 km south-west of Sūraj-Kuṇḍ, close to the village of Anangpur (also called Aṛangpur) is a dam ascribed to Anangpāl of the Tomar dynasty, who is also credited with the building of Lāl-Koṭ (p. 50). It can now also be reached by a road branching off west at a distance of about 19 km from Delhi on the Mathura road. Here, again, rain-water has been blocked by throwing up a dam of local quartzite stone across the mouth of a narrow ravine. The vast lake formed by the impounded waters is an impressive sight during the rainy months. The sluice openings in the dam allowed the water to flow through the ravine and irrigated the fields below.

In the neighbouring hills there exist also ruins of some fortifications, which lend support to the popular belief that Anangpur represents the site of a town founded by king Anangpāl.

31. TUGHLUQABAD AREA

A. Tughluqabad

The fortress of Tughluqabad (Tug͟hluqābād) stands on a rocky hill, about 8 km from the Qutb-Minar on the

Qutb-Badarpur road. Built by Ghiyāṯhu'd-Dīn Tughluq (1321-25), it constitutes the third city of Delhi. Roughly octagonal on plan with a perimeter of 6·5 km, its 10 to 15 m high rubble-built walls are provided with bastions and gates at intervals (pls. XII A). On its south was a vast reservoir created by erecting bunds between hills to its east. A causeway connected it with Ghiyāṯhu'd-Dīn's tomb, standing amidst waters, while a wide embankment near its south-eastern corner gave access to the fortress of 'Ādilābād, built a little later opposite it on another hill.

Tughluqabad was divided mainly into three portions. To the east of the present entrance from the Qutb-Badarpur road, a rectangular area with high walls and bastions served as the citadel. A wider area immediately to its west, similarly bounded by rubble walls and bastions, housed the palaces. Beyond this to the north lay the city, now marked by ruins of houses. Streets in the city, some of which can be traced even now, ran in a grid-pattern from gates on one side to those on the opposite side. Inside the citadel-enclosure are a tower known as Bijai-Manḍal and remains of several halls, including a long underground passage.

Near the embankment connecting it with 'Ādilābād are sluice gates through which water was controlled for irrigating the fields below.

B. Ghīyāṯhu'd-Dīn's tomb

Ghiyāṯhu'd-Dīn's self-built tomb, with a mausoleum enclosed within high battered pentagonal stone walls, strengthened with bastions, looks like a small fortress. Originally it stood within a vast reservoir and was connected with the fortress of Tughluqabad by a causeway, which has been pierced now by the Qutb-Badarpur road. The entrance to the tomb enclosure is through a high and massive gateway of red sandstone, approached by a flight of steps. The mausoleum, about 8 m sq, with sloping walls of red sandstone crowned with battlements is surmounted by a white marble dome raised on an octagonal drum. A string-course, inscribed panels, arch borders and perforated screens in tympana —all in marble—together with its 'lotus-bud' fringes break the monotony of the red sandstone and lend it a decorative effect (pl. XII B). There are three graves inside, the central one of Ghiyāthu'd-Dīn Tughluq and the other two believed to be those of his wife and his son and successor, Muḥammad bin Tughluq (1325-51).

Against the enclosure-walls are cells or pillared corridors with bracket-and-lintel openings. In the north-western bastion there is an octagonal tomb with an inscribed slab over its southern door, according to which one Ẓafar Khān lies buried in it. It seems that this tomb was the first to be raised here and while engaged on its construction, Ghiyāthu'd-Dīn had the idea of putting up an enclosure and siting his own tomb also inside it. The place is referred to as *Dāru'l-aman* ('abode of peace') in the inscription mentioned above and also in the contemporary accounts of Ghiyāthu'd-Dīn's tomb.

C. 'Ādilābād

The subsidiary fort of 'Ādilābād, south of Tughluqabad, was built by Ghiyāthu'd-Dīn's son and successor, Muhammad bin Tughluq (1325-51). Architecturally it is not much different from Tughluqabad. The walls of the embankment connecting it with Tughluqabad are carried over the hills as the outer walls of the city, and provided with two gates, one with barbicans between two bastions on the south-east and another on the south-west. Inside it, separated by a bailey, is a citadel consisting of walls, bastions and gates within which lay the palaces.

The fortress is also known as Muhammadābād and was perhaps built after Jahānpanāh (p. 73).

D. Nāi-kā-Koṭ

This small fortress in ruins, lies on a hillock to the east of 'Ādilābād. It is built in the same manner, but on a different plan, as the fortresses described above. Although known popularly as the fort of barber (*nāi*), or washerman or sweeper, it was probably built by Muḥammad bin Tughluq as a private residence before he constructed 'Ādilābād.

32. BUDHIĀWĀLA BRIDGE

The trunk road between the Indus and Sonargaon, built by Sher Shāh Sūr and maintained and improved by the Mughals, followed approximately the same alignment as the present Grand Trunk Road (p. 35). Among the bridges on the old road is the Buḍhiāwāla bridge over a stream, some 21 km from Delhi, a little to the east of the present Mathura road and now lying within the D.L.F. Industrial Estate.

Rubble-built and paved with stone, the bridge consists of three arched openings, with minarets on its parapets. Its present name is based on the tradition that in earlier days an old woman (*buḍhiā*) resided near it, while her sons were posted under it. She would beguile the travellers and drop an appropriate hint to her sons regarding the strength of the travellers. The sons would then overpower them and rob them of their valuables.

33. BADARPUR

About 17 km from Delhi on the Mathura road lies Badarpur one of the sarais built along the Grand Trunk Road, perhaps by Jahāngīr. It is enclosed by rubble-built walls consisting of two enclosures separated by a central gateway. There are high arched gateways also on the north and south through which the main road earlier passed.

34. AŚOKA'S ROCK-EDICT

This important record of the Maurya emperor Aśoka (273-36 B.C.), discovered in 1966, is engraved on a tilted rock-face in one of the outcrops near Srinivaspuri and may be approached from the Ring Road past Lajpatnagar. Consisting of ten lines in Brāhmī script and Prakrit language, the epigraph constitutes one of the versions of the emperor's Minor Rock Edicts and states that as a result of his exertions in the cause of *dhamma*, he had been able to bring the people of India (Jambudvīpa) closer to the gods. He appeals to his subjects, irrespective of whether they be men of importance or low station, to exert, so that they may attain heaven; for ever-enduring exertion would increase the quantum of attainment correspondingly and even more.

The situation of the epigraph, overlooking the Yamuna and not far from the ancient site of Purana-Qila, has clearly brought out the fact that not only was ancient Delhi an important town, it lay also on a trunk route connecting commercial centres and provincial capitals.

35. KALKAJI TEMPLE

Kalkaji temple, approached from Mathura road about 12 km. from Delhi by the side of the Okhla Industrial Estate or from the modern colony of Kalkaji, lies on a hill. It is of no architectural importance but is visited by worshippers and pilgrims and although built in the middle of the eighteenth century, it probably lies on an older site. The domed twelve-sided structure containing the stone representing the goddess Kālī (*piṇḍī*), known also as Kālikā, has been renovated from time to time.

36. HUMĀYŪN'S TOMB AREA

A. Humāyūn's Tomb

Humāyūn's tomb lies on the Mathura road near its crossing with the Lodi Road. High rubble-built walls enclose here a square garden divided initially into four large squares separated by causeways and channels, each square divided again into smaller squares by pathways (*chahārbāgh*) as in a typical Mughal garden. The lofty mausoleum is located in the centre of the enclosure and rises from a podium faced with series of cells with arched openings (pl. I). The central octagonal chamber containing the cenotaph is encompassed by octagonal chambers at the diagonals and arched lobbies on the sides, their openings closed with perforated screens. Each side is dominated by three emphatic arches, the central one being the highest. This plan is repeated on the second storey, and the roof is surmounted by a 42·5 m high double dome of marble with pillared kiosks (*chhatrīs*) placed around it. The structure is built with red sandstone, but white and black marble has been used to relieve the monotony, the latter largely in the borders.

The tomb was built by Humāyūn's senior widow Bega Begam, popularly known as Ḥājī Begam, nine years after his death in 1565 according to some, but fourteen years according to the manuscript of an eighteenth century text. It is the first substantial example of the Mughal architecture, with high arches and double dome, which occurs here for the first time in

India. Although some tombs had already been sited within gardens (pp. 94, 111), it is also the first mature example of the idea of garden-tomb, which culminated in the Tāj-Maḥal at Agra.

The enclosure is entered through two lofty double-storeyed gateways, one on the west and the other on the south, the latter now remaining closed. A *bāradarī* (pavilion) occupies the centre of the eastern wall of the enclosure and a bath-chamber that of the northern wall.

Several rulers of the Mug͟hal dynasty lie buried in the mausoleum, although it is not possible to identify their graves. Among those lying buried here are Bega Begam, Ḥamīdā Bānū Begam, Humāyūn's junior wife, Dāra S͟hikoh, S͟hāh Jahān's son, and the later Mug͟hals, Jahāndār S͟hāh, Farruk͟hsiyar, Rafī'u'd-Darajāt, Rafī'-u'd-Daula and 'Ālamgīr II, Bahādur S͟hah II, the last Mug͟hal emperor of Delhi, had taken shelter in this tomb with the three princes during the Mutiny and was captured here in 1857 by Lieutenant Hodson.

B. Barber's tomb

Within the compound of Humāyūn's tomb to its south-east stands an impressive square tomb with a double-dome. It is not quite known who is buried inside it, although it is usually referred to as Barber's tomb. There are two graves inside it inscribed with verses from the Quran. One of the graves is inscribed with the figure 999 which may stand for the Hijra year corresponding to 1590-91.

C. Nīla-Gumbad

Outside the Humāyūn's tomb enclosure on the south-eastern side stands an impressive tomb of plastered stone covered with a dome of blue tiles. Octagonal externally but square within, its ceiling is profusely decorated with painted and incised plaster. With its high neck and absence of a double dome which would be usual for this period, it is a unique construction. Conforming to its general colourful appearance around its drum are traces of tiles of other colours. Known as Nīla-Gumbad ('blue dome'), it is believed to have been built in 1625 by 'Abdu'r-Raḥīm Khān Khān-i-Khānān, and is said to contain the remains of Fahīm Khān, one of his faithful attendants. There is some indication, however, that the tomb may have existed even before the construction of Humāyūn's tomb and may, therefore, contain the remains of some other person.

D. Chilla-Nizāmu'd-dīn Auliya

Outside the north-eastern corner of Humāyūn's tomb are the remains of certain rooms with verandahs. It is believed that this place was used by Shaikh Niẓāmu'd-Dīn Auliya who died in 1325 and whose *dargāh* is described elsewhere (p. 115), although the constructional features of an adjacent double-storeyed house point out to its construction during the reign of Humāyūn or Akbar.

E. Arab-Sarai

The Arab-Sarai consists of a large enclosure adjoining the south-western corner of Humāyūn's tomb. It is divided into two quadrangles by series of cells provided with a gateway in the centre. The western enclosure has now been occupied by the Industrial Training Institute. Immediately outside its lofty eastern entrance approached by a gateway from the east, with traces of paintings on its underside, is the second quadrangle, originally bounded by arched cells, which is known as the *manḍī* (market) and was added by Mihr Bānū Āg͟ha, chief eunuch of Jahāngīr. The northern gate of the Arab-Sarai lies immediately to the right of the eastern gate of Bū'-Ḥalīma's garden.

It is said that the Arab-Sarai was built by Bega Begam or Hāji Begam for three hundred Arab *mullas* (priests) whom she had brought from Mecca. It is, however, suspected by some that the 'Arab-Sarai might possibly be a misnomer, and the enclosure probably housed Persian (not Arab) workers and craftsmen who were engaged in building Humāyūn's tomb.

F. Afsarwāla mosque and tomb

Within the eastern enclosure of the Arab-Sarai lies a mosque on a raised platform. Its prayer-chamber is faced by three arched openings, the central bay being roofed by a dome. In alignment with the mosque to its north is a long dilapidated hall with arched openings.

At the south-eastern corner of the mosque on the

same raised platform stands an octagonal tomb with double dome. The tomb and the mosque go under the name of Afsarwāla. The identity of the *afsar* or officer who raised these buildings is not known. One of the graves inside the tomb bears the figures 974, which may refer to Hijra year corresponding to 1566-67. Both the mosque and tomb may have been built about that time.

G. Bū'-Ḥalīma's Garden

As the visitor approaches Humāyūn's tomb from Mathura road, he passes through a rectangular enclosure with a tomb in its northern half and a gateway on its east, which is in the same alignment as the main entrance of Humāyūn's tomb. Since the northern wall of the Arab-Sarai abuts on the plastered exterior of the eastern enclosure of this garden, it may have existed before the Arab-Sarai, built by Humāyūn's senior widow. The garden is known as Bū'-Ḥalīma's garden, and an unidentified lady is believed to have been interred in the above-mentioned tomb. The coloured tiles, traces of which still exist on the entrance facing the Humāyūn's tomb, combined with the use of sandstone, both set in plaster, lend it a picturesque charm. It is doubtful, however, if the garden was originally laid for this tomb, as the latter is not in former's centre, as usual in garden-tombs.

H. 'Īsā Khān's tomb

'Īsā Khān's tomb (pl. XI B) stands immediately to the south of Bū'-Ḥalīma's garden. It consists of an octagonal garden enclosure, with entrance on the north, in the centre of which lies the mausoleum, as in Mubārak S͟hāh's tomb (p. 87). With a central octagonal chamber surrounded by verandahs, each side pierced by three arches, the mausoleum rises from a low plinth and is surrounded by a dwarf wall. Above the arches runs a *chhajja* and each of the side is surmounted on the roof by a domed *chhatrī*, with the central dome rising from a thirty-two-sided drum. The sides of the chamber are closed by perforated stone slabs except on the west and south. The western side contains a *miḥrāb* on the interior, while the southern side forms the main entrance. A three-domed mosque projects outward from the western side of the octagonal enclosure. It follows thus the typical pattern of the octagonal Lodī tombs.

'Īsā K͟hān was a nobleman at the courts of S͟her S͟hāh Sūr (1539-45) and his son Islām S͟hāh (1545-54). There is an inscription over the *miḥrāb* mentioning the date of 954 A.H. (1547-48).

I. BAṚA-BATĀS͟HEWĀLA-MAḤAL

Within an enclosure to the north of Humāyūn's tomb, now occupied by the Bharat Scouts and Guides, there are some monuments. The largest of these, known as Baṛa-Batās͟hewāla-Maḥal, stands on a raised platform, each of its sides pierced by five arches with a vaulted chamber in the centre. Originally it was surrounded by a walled enclosure, which has now disappeared.

Over the entrance to the central chamber is an inscription from which we learn that Mīrzā Muẓaffar was buried here in 1012 A.H. (1603). Mīrzā Muẓaffar Ḥusain, whose grandfather came from Khurasān to Bābur's court, was the son of Gulrukh Begam, daughter of Humāyūn's brother Mīrzā Kāmrān. He was married to the eldest daughter of Akbar, Sultan Khānam.

About 40 m east from Baṛa-Batāshewāla-Maḥal but within its original enclosure stands another rubble-built tomb with a central chamber, square within and octagonal externally, with floral, geometrical and inscriptional decoration in incised plaster on the interior. It is known as Chhoṭa-Baṭāshewāla-Maḥal. The identity of the person buried in the tomb is not known.

J. SABZ-BURJ

This octagonal tomb with four wide and four narrow sides (*muthamman-i-Baghdādī*), stands on the roundabout of the junction of Mathura road and Lodi road to the west of Humāyūn's tomb. It has high recessed arches on all its sides and a high-drummed double dome covered with coloured tiles, which has given it its present name, meaning the 'green dome'. Lacking such pre-Mughal features as *guldastas*, *chhajjas* and *chhatrīs*, architecturally, the building is in Central Asian tradition and can be placed in the early Mughal period. With traces of cross-walls on wheel-shaped plan and wooden beams preserved in the upper dome, it retains some clues of the methods of its construction.

K. NĪLĪ-CHHATRĪ

Nīlī-Chhatrī lies within the compound of the Delhi Public School on the Mathura road and is octagonal in plan. The building stood on a raised platform and was originally enclosed by a wall. Its outer façades were lavishly ornamented with enamelled tiles of several colours, but the entire superstructure has now been demolished. It is believed to be the tomb of Naubat K͟hān, a noble man of Akbar's court.

37. SUNDAR-BAGH NURSERY AREA

A. Sundarwāla-Maḥal and Burj

Within the present Sundar-Bagh Nursery existed originally a large enclosure entered through a lofty gateway. In its eastern portion stands a rubble-built tomb, rectangular in plan with chamfered corners and surmounted by a dome. Access to the chamber lies through the verandah with five arches on each of its four sides. Below the central chamber is an underground chamber, which must have contained a grave. There is considerable plaster decoration on the interior, which has now deteriorated.

It is known as Sundar-Maḥal or Sundarwāla-Maḥal. A domed square tomb profusely decorated with incised plaster on its inside stands in the western portion of the enclosure, and is called Sundar-Burj. The monuments belong to the early Mug͟hal period, but who lie buried in them is not known.

B. Lakkarwāla-Burj

Approached through the Sundar-Bagh Nursery to the north-west of Sundar-Burj is this rubble-built square domed tomb standing on a raised platform. The interior of the tomb is profusely decorated with floral and inscriptional designs in incised plaster. The identity of the person buried in it is not known.

38. NIZAMUDDIN

A. Ḥaẓrat Niẓāmu'd-Dīn's dargāh

Shaikh Nizāmu'd-Dīn was born at Budaun in 1236. He lost his father at the age of five and came to Delhi with his mother. Later he became the disciple of the famous saint Shaikh Farīd Shakarganj, who appointed him as his successor. Both 'Alāu'd-Dīn Khaljī (1296-1316) and Muḥammad Tughluq (1325-51) were devoted to him. He prophesied that Ghiyāthu'd-Dīn Tughluq, who was then in Bengal, would never see Delhi again and his prophecy came true, as the Sultan died in a temporary structure some 6 km south of Delhi.

Ḥaẓrat Niẓāmu'd-Dīn died in 1325. His original tomb does not exist any longer. It was repaired and decorated by Fīrūz Shāh Tughluq (1351-88), but even the repaired building has disappeared. The present structure was built in 970 A.H. (1562-63) by Farīdu'n Khān, a nobleman with a high rank, and has been added to or repaired later by several persons. It consists of a square chamber surrounded by verandahs, which are pierced by arched openings, while its roof is surmounted by a dome pringing from an octagonal drum. The dome is ornamented by vertical stripes of black marble and is crowned by a lotus-cresting. The area around the tomb is regarded as sacred, with the result that a large number of persons, including those from the royalty, lie buried here. Twice during the year, i.e. on the death anniversaries of Ḥaẓrat Niẓāmu'd-Dīn Auliya and Amīr Khusraw, a fair (*'urs*) is held here, when the entire area comes to life with pilgrims congregating from all over India.

B. Other monuments in the Dargāh

To the west of Ḥaẓrat Niẓāmu'd-Dīn's tomb lies the rectangular Jamā'at-Khāna-Masjid, veneered with red sandstone. Consisting of three bays, each surmounted by a low dome, the central one higher, its arches are fringed with the 'lotus-bud' decoration, recalling the features of the 'Alā'ī-Darwāza (p. 57). The mosque was built in 1325 by Khiẓr Khān, son of 'Alāu'd-Dīn Khaljī, and is the oldest building in this area. Khiẓr Khān was the hero of one of Amīr Khusraw's love-poems.

At the northern gate of the enclosure of the *dargāh* is a large *bāolī* (stepped well) which is considered sacred by the followers of the saint. It is said that the *bāolī* was under construction at the same time when Ghiyāthu'd-Dīn Tughluq was engaged in building Tughluqabad, and the latter had prohibited workmen to work elsewhere. They, however, worked for the saint at night and when the emperor forbade the sale of oil also, so that they could not work during the nights, they used the water of the *bāolī* for oil, and it served the purpose equally well.

On the western wall of the *bāolī*, a mosque called Chīnī-kā-Burj, consists of three compartments, each with an arched opening. An inscription incised in plaster in a domed chamber on its roof is too fragmentary to be made out. The building was, however, apparently built in the Lodī times. The profuse decoration with coloured tiles and incised plaster on the interior of its upper chamber has given it its present name of Chīnī-kā-Burj, meaning a 'tower of tiles'. On the same side of the *bāolī* stands a small marble pavilion with a vaulted roof and three arched entrances. It is known as Bāi-Kodaldāi's tomb, but who this lady was is not known.

To the south of Shaikh Niẓāmu'd-Dīn's tomb is situated the unroofed enclosure with perforated marble screens containing the grave of Jahānārā, Shāh Jahān's elder daughter. The hollow receptacle on the grave is filled with grass in accordance with the touching inscription on it, meaning 'Let naught cover my grave save the green grass: for grass well suffices as a covering for the grave of the lowly'. The tomb of Muḥammad Shāh (1719-48) also lies within a small enclosure similar to Jahānārā's tomb. Mīrzā Jahāngīr, the eldest son of Akbar II (1806-37), also lies buried in an enclosure here.

South of the above-mentioned tombs is Amīr Khusraw's tomb, which bears inscriptions of several dates. Amīr Khusraw, the chief disciple of Shaikh Niẓāmu'd-Dīn Auliya, enjoyed the patronage of several rulers and was a celebrated saint and poet.

C. Kālī- or Kalān-Masjid

On the eastern periphery of the village of Nizamuddin lies Kālī- or Kalān-Masjid, built by Khān-i-Jahān Jūnān Shāh, prime minister of Fīrūz Shāh Tughluq (1351-88). It is one of the seven mosques reputed to have been built by him (p. 27). Built of rubble stone, it is an extensive structure. Originally its courtyard was partly covered and partly uncovered as in the Khiṛkī-Masjid (p. 75). Its eastern doorway has an inscription mentioning that it was built in 772 A.H. (1370-71) by Jūnān Shāh Maqbūl, entitled Khān-i-Jahān, son of Khān-i-Jahān.

D. Khān-i-Jahān Tilangānī's tomb

In the north-western corner of the village stands the tomb of Khān-i-Jahān Tilangānī, the prime minister of Fīrūz Shāh Tughluq (1351-88), his real name being Khān-i-Jahān Maqbūl Khān (p. 27). It consists of a central octagonal chamber enclosed by a verandah and covered by a dome. Each of its sides is pierced by three arched openings. Although now in a dilapidated condition, architecturally it occupies an important place in the development of tombs, being the first octagonal tomb in Delhi (p. 27).

E. Ataga Khān's tomb

The northern periphery of the village of Nizamuddin is occupied by a small tomb built of red sandstone within a walled enclosure. On all its four sides are deeply recessed arches containing openings and its red sandstone facing is thickly inlaid with marble and coloured tiles. Its interior was ornamented with painted plaster, which has now largely come off. Coloured tiles are also fixed on the western wall of its enclosure containing recessed arches. Although small in size, measuring 6 m sq., it is virtually a gem of architecture.

Ataga Khān was the husband of Jī Jī Anga, a wet nurse of Akbar and held important positions in the court. In 1562 he was killed by Adham Khān, son of Māham Anga, another wet nurse of Akbar. An inscription on the southern door of the tomb mentions that it was finished in 974 A.H. (1566-67).

F. Chaunsath-Khambā

Not far from Ataga Khān's tomb to its east lies the Chaunsaṭh-Khambā, a marble pavilion with sixty-four pillars. It contains several graves including that of Mīrzā 'Azīz Kokaltāsh, Ataga Khān's son. Built earlier as a hall, it may have been converted later into a tomb. It is surrounded by an enclosure wall, but is sited within the raised western half of the enclosure. The main grave is inscribed and bears the date 1033 A.H. (1623-24).

G. Ghālib's tomb

Outside the enclosure of Chaunsaṭh-Khambā on its north lies the grave of the famous poet Mīrzā Ghālib (1796-1869). In recent years the grave has been covered by a small marble structure and enclosed within a compound wall.

H. Bārā-Khambā

North of the village of Nizamuddin stands a large square structure consisting of a central chamber with three arches on each side and supported on twelve sets of pillars, from which it has derived its present name meaning 'twelve pillars'. Around the central chamber on all the sides runs a verandah. Originally it appears to have been a tomb, the identity of the person buried in it being unknown.

I. Lāl-Maḥal

Outside Chaunsaṭh-Khambā a red sandstone building in private occupation, now considerably renovated, attracts attention. Known as Lāl-Maḥal or 'red palace', it has a central domed room, with verandahs on all the sides. The verandahs have a flat roof supported on pillars and lintels. It is identified sometimes with Kushk-i-Lāl ('red palace'), built by Ghiyāthu'd-Dīn Balban (1266-86), which, however, remains untraced.

J. Khān-i-Khānān's tomb

The tomb of 'Abdu'r-Raḥīm Khān, who had the title of Khān-i-Khānān, lies on the east of Mathura road opposite Nizamuddin. It is a massive square edifice rising from a high platform faced by arched cells (pl. XX B). Double-storyed, with a high deeply recessed central arch on each side and several shallow arches on the flanks in each storey, it follows the pattern of Humāyūn's tomb. The interior of the tomb is decorated with incised and painted plaster with beautiful designs, specially on the ceiling. Around the central double dome are disposed *chhatrīs* at the corners and *dālāns* (open halls) in the middle of the sides. The red sandstone, marble and other stones which faced it originally were later removed and used in Safdar-Jang's tomb (p. 89).

'Abdu'r Rahīm Khān Khān-i-Khānān was the son of Bairam Khān, regent of Akbar, and served both Akbar and Jahāngīr. He knew several languages and composed couplets in Hindi under the familiar name of Rahīm. He died in 1626-27.

K. Bārāpula

Bārāpula is a bridge on the old Mathura road, 1 km east of Khān-i-Khānān's tomb. It consists of eleven arched openings, but twelve piers which appear to have given it its name meaning 'twelve piers' (p. 95). Each pier is surmounted by a 2 m high *mīnār*. The bridge is 14 m in width and over 195 m in length. There was an inscription on one of its arches, now not traceable, according to which, it was built in 1030 A.H. (1621-22) by Mihr Bānū Āgha, the chief eunuch of Jahāngīr's court.

39. LĀL-BANGLA

Near the entrance to the Delhi Golf Club on the Dr Zakir Husain Road (old Wellesley Road) lie two tombs of red sandstone. They consist of a square room in the centre, smaller square rooms at the diagonals and oblong halls between them. One of the tombs contains two graves believed to be that of Lāl Kunwar, mother of S̲h̲āh 'Ālam II (1759-1806) and Begam Jan, his daughter. Originally there existed another tomb, later converted to its use by the Golf Club, and all the three tombs were enclosed within a compound wall. It is not quite certain whether the name of Lāl Kunwar or the use of red (*lāl*) sandstone in the buildings has given it the name of Lāl-Bangla ('red bungalow').

40. PURANA-QILA AREA

A. Purana-Qila

The Purana-Qila (Purāna-Qal'a) occupies the ancient mound which conceals perhaps the ruins of the city of Indraprastha of *Mahābhārata* story (p. 8). S̲h̲er S̲h̲āh Sūr (1538-45) demolished the city of Dīnpanāh built by Humāyūn and on the same site raised this citadel. It is irregularly oblong on plan, with bastions on the corners and in the western wall. Its ramparts cover a perimeter of nearly 2 km. It has three main gates on the north, south and west, the last one functioning as the entrance now. The gates are double-storeyed, built with red sandstone and surmounted by *chhatrīs*. On the inside, against the enclosure wall run cells in two-bay depth.

Among the three main gates, the northern one is called the Talāqī-Darwāza ('forbidden gate'). Why and when the entrance through it was forbidden is not known. Above the oriel windows on its front are carved marble leogryphs engaged in combat with a man. The exterior of the gate was originally decorated with coloured tiles, and the rooms with incised plaster-work. It is believed that Sher Shāh left the Purana-Qila unfinished, and it was completed by Humāyūn. Among the scribblings in ink that existed in a recess of the gate, there was a mention of Humāyūn, and it is possible, therefore, that if the gate was not constructed by Humāyūn, it was at least repaired by him. In the southern gate, which is called the Humāyūn-Darwāza, there existed a similar inscription in ink mentioning Sher Shāh and the date 950 A.H. (1543-44).

Purana-Qila originally lay on the bank of the Yamuna. The general depression on the northern and western sides of the fortress suggests that a wide moat connected with the river existed on these sides, which were approached through a causeway connecting the fortress with the main land.

B. Excavated site

In 1955, in some trial trenches sunk in the south-eastern portion of the Purana-Qila, pieces of the Painted Grey Ware turned up, apart from relics and remains of later periods. Since this characteristic ware had been noticed earlier at several sites associated with the story of the *Mahābhārata* and had been dated to around 1000 B.C., its occurence here seemed to support the tradition of Purana-Qila being the site of Indraprastha, capital of the Pāṇḍavas, heroes of the *Mahābhārata*.

Excavations (pl. XXI) were resumed here in 1969 along the flanks of the passage leading to the Water Gate in the eastern wall and continued till 1973. A settlement of the Painted Grey Ware people has not been located, but a continuous stratification from the Mauryan to Early Mughal period has certainly emerged. Pieces of the Painted Grey Ware occur, however, sporadically, but among later deposits. Evidence of the Mauryan Period (*c.*300 B.C.) is provided by the existence of the Northern Black Polished Ware, a fine hard earthen pottery with a glossy surface, punch-marked coins, human and animal terracotta figurines and inscribed terracotta seals. Soak-wells lined with terracotta rings and burnt bricks have also been found, although most of the dwellings were made of mud bricks or wattle and daub, sometimes reinforced with wooden posts.

The Northern Black Polished Ware continued during the Śuṅga Period (*c.* 200-100 B.C.) along with plain red pottery. The houses were largely built of local rubble or of mud bricks over rubble foundations. Tamped earth or mud bricks made up the floors. The characteristic art of this period, reflecting the religious beliefs of people, is represented by small terracotta plaques modelling semi-divine beings (*yakṣas* and *yakṣīs*). Uninscribed cast coins of the Mathura kings and terracotta sealings also occur in these levels.

Stamped decoration marks the red earthenware

of the next Śaka-Kushan Period (*c.* 100 B.C.-A.D. 300). Firm evidence of the chronology of this period is provided by the copper currency of the Yaudheyas and Kushans. The increasing use of burnt brick appears now to lend an urban look to the settlement.

Surprisingly, in the levels of the succeeding Gupta Period (*c.* 400-600) the houses that have been encountered are built of brickbats. A gold-plated coin with the figure of an archer on the obverse and the legend *Śrī-Vikrama* on the reverse leaves no doubt that it belongs to one of the Gupta rulers. Inscribed sealings and beautifully modelled human figurines are other characteristic objects of this period. A coarse red earthenware, terracotta figurines and pieces of fine but damaged stone sculpture indicate the occupation of the site during the Post-Gupta Period (*c.* 700-800).

Towards the end of the Rajput Period (*c.* 900-1200) a massive rubble wall was raised to enclose perhaps part of the town, although the houses continued to be built with rubble, brickbats and mud bricks. There was little change in pottery. Coins of 'bull and horseman' type, including those of Sāmanta Deva, have also been recovered from these levels.

During the succeeding Sultanate rule (1206-1526), rubble and brickbats were used for ordinary houses. But it witnessed the introduction of glazed ware, both of Central Asian affinities and local manufacture. Coins of Balban (1266-1286) and Muḥammad bin Tug̱hluq (1325-51) have turned up in these levels. Typical and fascinating objects of the Early Mug̱hal Period (1526-1556), representing the rule of Bābur, Sūrs and Humāyūn, came from a refuse dump of discarded broken household objects. These included jars of eggshell-thin grey ware, glazed ware dishes and painted Chinese porcelain, a piece of which bears the Chinese inscription 'made in the great Ming Dynasty of the Cheng Hua era' (1465-87). On another piece is inscribed a fairy tale in Chinese verse. Other interesting objects comprised glass wine bottles, a gold ear-ring inlaid with emerald and pearls and a coin of 'Ādil Shāh Sūr (1552-53).

C. Qal'a-i-Kuhna-Masjid

Among the few buildings still extant within the Purana-Qila is the Qal'a-i-Kuhna-Masjid ('mosque of the old fort'), built by Sher Shāh in 1541 (pl. XVIII A) Its prayer-hall measures 51·20 m by 14·90 m, and is fronted by five openings with horseshoe-shaped arches. The central arch, higher than the others and framed within a projection, is flanked by narrow fluted pilasters. The recessed surface of the arch, through which there is an opening, is beautifully decorated with inlay of marble and other stones and contains a small oriel window at its apex. The two arches on either side are similarly treated but with less of ornamentation. In the arches at the ends plain grey stone is used instead of the red stone. The *miḥrābs* inside the hall are richly decorated with concentric arches which enhance the scope for ornamentation. The rear-corners rise with double-storeyed towers and oriel windows. From both the ends in the hall staircases lead to a narrow passage on the second storey running right round the rectangular hall. The central bay of the hall is surmounted by a beautiful dome, with traces of *chhatrīs* on either side. In the courtyard originally existed a shallow tank provided with a fountain.

This mosque occupies an important position in the development of the mosque, exemplifying the transition from the Lodī to Mughal styles. The façade of five arches, oriel windows and corner-towers at the rear are features which have developed from the earlier mosques such as the Baṛā-Gumbad-Masjid (p.92), Moṭh-Masjid (p. 78) and Jamālī-Kamālī-Masjid (p. 66).

D. Sher-Manḍal

To the south of the Qal'a-i-Kuhna-Masjid is a double-storeyed octagonal tower of red sandstone relieved by marble. It is surmounted by an octagonal pavilion or *chhatrī*. On each of its sides is a recessed arch in the centre. On the second storey the central chamber is cruciform, with recesses on its four sides. The dados of its interior are decorated with glazed tiles, while the upper portion contains incised and painted plaster-work.

The purpose of the building is not very certain. It may have been built by Sher Shāh as a pleasure resort, but is believed to have been used as a library by Humāyūn, from the steps of which he fell down and ultimately met his end (p. 38).

E. Khairu'l-Manāzil-Masjid

In front of the Purana-Qila on the other side of the Mathura road stands the Khairu'l-Manāzil-Masjid ('the most auspicious of houses'), a rubble-built structure with five arched openings in its prayer-hall, double-storeyed cloisters and an imposing gateway of red sandstone on the east. The central bay of the prayer-hall is provided with a dome, the other bays being roofed with vaults. Originally the façade of the prayer-chamber was profusely decorated with enamelled tiles. The double-storeyed corridors were used as a *madrasa*.

Over the central arch of the prayer-chamber is an inscription, from which we learn that it was built by Māham Anga, with the assistance of Shihā-bu'd-Dīn Aḥmad Khān during the reign of Akbar.

The mosque was built in 1561. Māham Anga was one of the wet-nurses of Akbar and held considerable influence over him. Her son, Adham Khān was a nobleman and a general in Akbar's army, whose tomb is described elsewhere (p. 60). Shihā-bu'd-Dīn Aḥmad Khān was a relation and friend of Māham Anga and a powerful courtier, who held the position of the governor of Delhi at one time.

F. Sher Shāh gate

By the side of Khairu'l-Manāzil-Masjid to its north lies one of the gates believed to be an entrance to the extensive city of Delhi built by Sher Shāh sprawling in front of his citadel of Purana-Qila. The gate is largely built with red sandstone with some use of local grey quartzite in its upper storey, and is, therefore, also known as Lāl-Darwāza. Later the arcades from this gate into the city appear to have been provided with series of apartments fronted by a verandah, which were possibly used as shops. Another gate on the periphery of Sher Shāh's extensive city is said to be the Kābulī- or Khūnī-Darwāza (p. 132).

41. 'ABDU'N NABĪ'S MOSQUE

'Abdu'n Nabī's mosque, about 400 m north of the Tilak bridge, lies with its back on the Mathura road. It is a rubble-built structure consisting of a prayer-hall entered through three arched openings, the central apartment of which is provided with a dome. The cloisters on the sides of its courtyard have disappeared. Originally there was an inscription above the main arched bay of the prayer-hall, from which it is learnt that it was built by Shaikh 'Abdu'n Nabī in 983 A.H. (1575-76). The façade of the prayer-hall was originally decorated with coloured tiles which have largely disappeared. The original features of the mosque have suffered during its recent renovation.

'Abdu'n Nabī held the post of Sadar, a kind of ecclesiastical registrar, in Akbar's reign and enjoyed his confidence. He was sent by the emperor to Mecca with money for distribution to the poor, but on his return he failed to account for the money and was put in prison and murdered in 1584-85.

42. KOTLA FIROZ SHAH

A. Ramparts and gates

According to contemporary historians Fīrūzābād, the fifth city of Delhi built by Fīrūz Shāh Tughluq

(1351-88), extended from Hauz-Khas to Pīr-Ghāib (p. 135) in the north, although no remains of any large city-wall to answer to such a size have been traced. Kotla Firoz Shah, then lying along the banks of the Yamuna, and now situated on the Mathura road outside the Delhi Gate of Shāhjahānābād, served as its citadel and was called Kushk-i-Fīrūz, i.e., Fīrūz's palace. It consists of three rubble-built walled rectangular enclosures, with their eastern wall in one alignment. The central enclosure is larger than the other two, one on the north and the other on the south, which have a set-back on the west. The northern enclosure can be traced only in part, having been largely covered by modern structures. The southern enclosure, with an extant independent gateway, now encloses the Vikramnagar colony.

The main gateway to the central enclosure from the west is flanked by a bastion on either side and was fronted by a barbican. There are also the remains of a gateway from the northern enclosure, a similar gateway from the southern enclosure having been later closed. In addition, several flights of steps from the terrace above the eastern wall lead down to the old river bank. The ramparts, provided with bastions in the corners, are pierced by loop-holes, without, however, a platform on which the arrow-dischargers could stand. Such a platform, if it existed, may have been removed later.

B. Jāmi'-masjid

Among the few surviving buildings inside the citadel is the Jāmi'-Masjid, ascended by a gateway on the north.

It rests on a series of cells on the ground floor. The cloisters on the sides of its courtyard and its prayer-hall have disappeared, with only a rear wall standing on the western side. The Jāmi'-Masjid was one of the largest mosques in the Tughluq times. Tīmūr mentions having visited it to say his prayers.

C. Pyramidal structure and Aśokan pillar

A lofty rubble-built structure in three storeys, with size diminishing in each successive storey, consisting of cells with arched entrances, lies to the north of the Jāmi'-Masjid (pl. XIV A). On its top terrace is installed the Aśokan column from Topra in Ambala District, which was brought by Fīrūz Shāh and fixed here (p. 26). Originally it appears to have been enclosed within stone railings. The Aśokan edicts on this column were the first to be deciphered in 1837 by James Prinsep yielding the key to the Brāhmī script. The other column brought by Fīrūz Shāh from the neighbourhood of Meerut is fixed on the ridge (p. 136). Contemporary historians describe the complicated operation adopted for bringing these pillars to Delhi by the river, without much damage to them.

D. Other monuments

The contemporary historians name several palaces in the citadel, but none of these has been identified. There are remains of several structures to the south of the Jāmi'-Masjid, including a tower with holes for pigeons. Some of these appear to be residential. To the north-west of the pyramidal structure is a fine circular *bāolī*, with a range of subterranean apartments and a large drain leading from its upper levels towards the eastern side.

43. KĀBULĪ- OR KHŪNĪ-DARWĀZA

Right on the Mathura road near Maulana Azad Medical College stands a double-storeyed imposing gate, built largely with grey stone, red stone having been used in the frames of its windows. It is believed to be one of the gates of Sher Shāh's city of Delhi (p. 35), although no remains of a city-wall have been traced in continuation with it. Another surviving gate of the city has been described earlier (p. 128).

It is also known as Lāl-Darwāza. It derives the name Khūnī-Darwāza ('bloody gate'), from the tradition that two of Bahādur Shāh's sons were hanged here.

44. HASHTSAL-MĪNĀR

The small village of Hashtsal lies at the end of the narrow approach road from its junction with Delhi-Najafgarh road, 17 km from Delhi, on the bank of a lake—a vast depression which gets filled with water during the rains. Inside the village is a three-storeyed brick-built tapering *mīnār*, 17 m high, faced with red stone, with a narrow staircase leading to its top. It rises from a two-tiered platform, the lower one square and the upper one octagonal. The lower half of its first storey is twelve-sided, the remaining height being provided alternatively with angular and semi-circular flutings as in the third storey of the Qutb-Minar (p. 53).

About 100 m to its north-west are the remains of a double-storeyed pavilion, called Hāthī-Khāna ('elephant-stable'). It is believed that Shāh Jahān built the pavilion as a hunting lodge. The *mīnār* may have been intended by him to be used as a shooting-tower.

45. QADAM-SHARĪF

Qadam-Sharīf lies in Paharganj and may be reached either from the Qutb Road along the railway line or from the crossing of the Chitragupta and Originals roads. It is believed that the large square tomb here was built by Fīrūz Tughluq (1351-88) for his own use, but when his son prince Fatḥ Khān died, he utilised it for interring the latter's remains.

According to tradition Fīrūz Shāh's spiritual guide, Makhdūm Jahāniān Jahān Gasht brought from Mecca at the emperor's order, a stone with the Prophet's footprint (*qadam*) and as Fatḥ Khān died before his father, it was placed at his grave. The emperor later built a mosque and school here, and enclosed the tomb within high battlemented walls.

Adjacent to the tomb were later added several chambers, such as the Majlis-Khāna ('assembly hall') and Langar-Khāna ('feeding house'). There are also several graves and tombs inside the enclosure.

46. GHĀZĪU'D-DĪN KHĀN'S COLLEGE AND TOMB

These monuments lie outside the Ajmeri Gate of Shāhjahānābād. They consist of a large enclosure of arcaded apartments with a gate on the east and a three-domed mosque on the west, with an enclosure of perforated stone screens, both on the latter's north and south. Ghāzīu'd-Dīn Khān's grave is one of the three in the southern enclosure. Red sandstone has been used as facing veneer in most of the monuments.

Ghāzīu'd-Dīn Khān was an influential courtier during the reigns of Aurangzeb (1658-1707) and his son and ultimate successor Shāh 'Ālam I (1707-12). His son, Mīr Qamaru'd-Dīn was appointed the governor of the Deccan by Muḥammad Shāh (1719-48) and became the founder of the dynasty of the Nizam of Hyderabad.

The arcaded apartments were used as a *madrasa*, which became first the Anglo-Arabic School and later the Anglo-Arabic College, and is now known as the Delhi College.

47. NORTHERN RIDGE

A. Flagstaff tower

The crest of the northern part of the Ridge near the University is occupied by a circular tower, originally surmounted by a flagstaff. It commemorates the site where the British ladies and children gathered on the 11th May 1857, during the Mutiny, before they fled to Karnal. It is also the site where the rebels made their last stand on the 8th June 1857 before falling back behind the city walls.

B. Chauburjī-Masjid

About 400 m south-east of the Flagstaff Tower lies the Chauburjī-Masjid, a double-storeyed structure with a central chamber surrounded by a small chamber on each side. There is a *miḥrāb* in the west wall of the western chamber. The upper storey is occupied by a domed chamber on the south-west corner, other such chambers having disappeared. It derives its name, meaning the 'mosque with four towers', from its original four domes. It was repaired and altered in the late Mughal times.

It was built by Fīrūz Shāh Tughluq (1351-88), evidently as a mausoleum and probably formed part of his palace called Kuskh-i-Shikār or Kushk-i-Jahān-Numā by contemporary writers. Another surviving part of his palace is Pīr-Ghāib described below.

C. Pīr-Ghāib

Some distance south-west of the Chauburjī-Masjid is a double-storeyed dilapidated rubble-built structure, now falling within the compound of the Hindu Rao Hospital, with a *bāolī* in its neighbourhood. Among its surviving remains exist two narrow chambers giving access from the east and west, with other rooms on the north and south. There are two rooms on the second storey with openings on the east and *miḥrābs* in the western wall, with pious exclamations incised above them on plaster. They appear to have been used as a mosque. In the northern apartment a cenotaph lying east to west, commemorates, according to tradition, a saint who used this room as his *c̲h̲illāgāh* (worshipping place) but disappeared at last mysteriously (*g̲h̲āib*), from which the monument has derived its present name meaning the 'vanished saint'.

The floor and the roof of the southern apartment are pierced by a hole, covered by a hollow masonry cylinder. Its purpose is not known, but it is believed to have been used for astronomical observations and may have some connection with the description of the place as Kus̲h̲k-i-Jahān-Numā ('world-showing palace') found in contemporary accounts. The structure was built by Fīrūz S̲h̲āh Tug̲h̲luq and forms part either of his Kus̲h̲k-i-S̲h̲ikār ('hunting palace') or Kus̲h̲k-i-Jahān-Numā. S̲h̲arfu'd-Dīn 'Alī Yāzdī mentions that Tīmūr visited Fīrūz S̲h̲āh's palace, called Jahān-Numā.

D. Aśoka's pillar

Between the Chauburjī-Masjid and Hindu Rao Hospital on the north of the road is set up the Aśokan pillar, which was brought by Fīrūz S̲h̲āh Tug̲h̲luq from the neighbourhood of Meerut and erected at his hunting palace. The other pillar brought by him from Topra was set up in Kotla Firoz Shah (p. 131).

The pillar bears Aśoka's Edicts, I-V, partly or almost fully. The contemporary historians describe the complicated transport of these pillars from their original site to Delhi by the river. The pillar measures now 10 m in length. It broke into five pieces in an explosion during Farrukhsiyar's reign (1713-19) and its inscribed portions were later sawed off and sent to the Asiatic Society of Bengal at Calcutta. In 1866 they were received back and all the pieces erected here in 1867.

E. Ajitgarh or Mutiny Memorial

About 200 m south of Asoka's pillar, approached by another road, is the Mutiny Memorial, recently rechristened as Ajitgarh. An octagonal tapering tower of red stone rising from a two-tiered platform and provided with a staircase on the interior, it occupies the site of Taylor's Battery during the seige of Delhi in 1857, and was built in 1863 in the memory of the soldiers of the Delhi Field Force who were killed during the Mutiny.

The names of different units, officers and the number of the British and Indian officers and ranks who were killed in the Mutiny are inscribed on different slabs around the tower. Earlier it was known as Fatehgarh or Jitgarh. But in 1972 on the twenty-fifth anniversary of India's attainment of freedom, a new plaque has been fixed here, and the site converted into a memorial for those martyrs who rose against colonial rule in 1857.

48. SHĀLIMĀR GARDEN

A narrow road branching off west from the Delhi-Karnal road about 10 km from Delhi, just beyond Badli-Sarai, leads to the village of Haidarpur. About 800 m east of the village lies the Shālimār garden, where Aurangzeb crowned himself on the 31st July, 1658 (p. 46). Originally it consisted of an enclosure with a palace in the centre, called Shīsh-Maḥal, now surviving in parts with patches of painting. There were also some other buildings, but they have all disappeared.

Originally the garden was known as 'Aizzābād-Bāgh. It was perhaps built by Shāh Jahān and named after his mistress 'Aizzu'n-Nisā Begam. Aurangzeb used it as his country-house. It has been mentioned by European travellers like Bernier and Catrou. Sir David Ochterlony, British Resident at Delhi, used it as his summer retreat and contracted fever here from which he ultimately died.

49. BADLI-SARAI

About 10 km from Delhi on the Delhi-Karnal road lies Badli, where a sarai was built in the late Mughal times. The enclosure of the sarai, with its arcaded rooms has disappeared, but its two gateways through which the Grand Trunk Road originally passed still stand.

On the same side of the road, about 500 m north is the sandstone column put up in the memory of the Gordon Highlanders who fell here during the Mutiny. On the opposite side of the road is a small octagonal tomb, called Maqbara-Pāik, with arched recesses on all the sides, but openings only on the cardinal points.

50. CORONATION MEMORIAL

About 17 km from Delhi on Bhai Parmanand Road branching off north from the Mall (Karnal road) from the roundabout at Kingsway stands the Coronation Memorial, a sandstone pillar, where a *Darbār* was held in 1911 on the occasion of the visit of King GeorgeV and Queen Mary.

51. TRIPOLIA GATEWAYS

On the road connecting Subzimandi with the present Delhi-Karnal road was a sarai called Guṛ-kī-Sarai built in the late Mughal times. The old Grand Trunk Road passed through its triple gateways with arched openings at either end. Largely built with brick, with use of sandstone in dressings, these gates were built by Nāẓir Maḥaldār Khān in 1141 A.H. (1728-29), as learnt from two inscriptions, one over each gateway.

52. RAUSHANĀRĀ'S GARDEN AND TOMB

The tomb of Raushanārā, younger daughter of Shāh Jahān, who died in 1671, lies about 400 m south of the Clock-Tower in Subzimandi. She laid out her garden-tomb in 1650, soon after the completion of Shāhjahānābād (p. 142) by her father. Lying in the middle of the garden, which has seen several alterations in its layout, the tomb, popularly known as Bārādarī, consists of a brick-built but plastered small roofless grave-chamber in the centre surrounded by a hall, the four sides of which are occupied by arcaded *dālāns* (apartments with arched openings), with double-storeyed domed chambers on the corners. Originally the tomb was enclosed by deep ornamental troughs provided with fountains on either side. They fell into disuse and were covered by platforms, but have been latterly exposed. In recent years gardens have been laid out here in Japanese style.

53. WAZIRABAD

The village of Wazirabad lies on the bank of the Yamuna a little beyond Timarpur, which is reached by a road branching off north from the Mall, about 6 km from Delhi. Tīmūr encamped near Wazirabad on his return journey from Delhi and crossed the Yamuna near it.

About one km south of the village at the crossing of a *nullah* which falls into the Yamuna lie some rubble-built monuments, erected by Fīrūz Shāh Tughluq (1351-88). The principal monument is a mosque, with its two-bay deep prayer-chamber, pierced by five arches. The rear bay is surmounted by three domes, while a small chamber supported on pillars and screened with perforated slabs has been raised as an intermediate storey for the use of ladies.

In the centre of the courtyard of the mosque enclosed by walls is a square tomb, said to be of Shāh 'Ālam, a saint of Fīrūz Tughluq's time. Its domed roof rests on twelve pillars, and its sides were originally closed by perforated screens, some of them still surviving.

The *nullah* is spanned by a rubble-built bridge of nine arched openings, with a solid causeway running in continuation to its north. There are three small bays at its northern end, with a sluice chamber, which has sometimes been taken as a fish-trap.

54. METCALFE HOUSE

Below the Ridge and approached by the Mahatma Gandhi Road (old Metcalfe Road) from its junction with the Alipur road, lies the Metcalfe House consisting of several apartments in early Indo-European style, built in about 1835 by Sir Thomas Metcalfe, Resident at the Mughal court. He died in this house in 1853. Later it was occupied by his son and successor, Sir Theophilus Metcalfe, who was born at Delhi, and played an important role during the Mutiny. The Metcalfe House finds mention in several contemporary descriptions and diaries as a place of social parties.

The House was sold by Sir Theophilus Metcalfe and, after changing hands several times, ultimately it came to the Government of India, and now houses a Government office.

55. QUDSIYA-BAGH

Nawab Quḍsiya Begam, originally a dancing-girl, who became a favourite mistress of Muḥammad

Shāh (1719-48), and was mother of Aḥmad Shāh (1748-54), built a large garden on the bank of the Yamuna in about 1748 now lying immediately to the north of the Kashmiri Gate. The palace and other buildings originally laid out in the garden have disappeared. Its lofty western gateway, which served as the main entrance, however, still stands. About 300 m to its east lies a mosque, with three arched openings and surmounted by three domes. The mosque was repaired in 1249 A.H. (1833-34) by Bahādur Shāh II who has left a dated inscription on a marble slab in the northern wall of the prayer-chamber.

56. SHĀHJAHĀNĀBĀD

A. Ramparts and gateways

Shāh Jahān transferred his capital from Agra to Delhi in 1638 and laid the foundation of Shāhjahānābād, the seventh city of Delhi, which was completed in 1649. The city, polygonal in plan, was provided with houses in blocks, wide roads, mosques and bazars, among which Chandni-Chowk, with a tree-shaded channel flowing in its centre, was one of the most enchanting markets in the contemporary East. With the Red Fort at its north-eastern base, the city was engirdled by rubble-built high walls strengthened by bastions, circular as well as square, and pierced by several gates. Large portions of the city-walls suffered damage later during the Mutiny and were rebuilt. Over some of its parts the wall has disappeared only in recent years, but substantial stretches of it still survive.

Of its main fourteen gates, apart from wicket-entrances, only some have escaped demolition. Among these are Ajmeri Gate on the south-west, Turkman Gate on the south (approached from the Jawahar Lal Nehru Road, old Circular Road), Kashmiri Gate on the north, Nigambodh Gate on the north-east and Delhi Gate on the south-east. These gates, square on plan, are pierced by high arched openings, except the Nigambodh gate, which is low, and the Kashmiri Gate, which has lateral double openings, one for the entrance and the other for exit.

B. Kālī- or Kalān-Masjid

Kālī- or Kalān-Masjid is reached from the Turkman Gate and is one of the seven mosques reputed to have been built by Khān-i-Jahān Jūnān Shāh, son of a father with the same title and prime minister of Fīrūz Shāh Tughluq (1351-88). With a basement faced by series of double apartments, its courtyard is enclosed within domed arcaded cloisters and is reached by a high flight of steps on the east. Its prayer-chamber is three-aisle deep, and pierced by five openings, each bay surmounted by a low dome.

Among the four graves in its courtyard removed in 1857, two were said to be those of the builder and his father (see also pp. 27, 118). An inscription over its eastern entrance states that the mosque was built in 789 A.H. (1387) by Jūnān Shāh Maqbūl, entitled Khān-i-Jahān, son of Khān-i-Jahān.

C. Sultana Raẓiya's tomb

Iltutmish's able and valiant daughter Rẓaiya ascended the throne in 1236 and was the only woman to rule over Delhi. Later she faced revolt by her nobles and fled to Kaithal in Karnal District, where she is believed to have been captured, killed and buried (p. 20). But a plain tomb to the east of the Kālī-Masjid, reached by a forking lane within Shāhjahānābād some distance inside the Turkman Gate, is believed to be her tomb by tradition. It is an unroofed walled enclosure of rubble-stone, with two graves in the centre and another two in the south-west corner. The central graves are said to contain the remains of Raẓiya and her sister Saẓiya, who is unknown to history.

D. Zīnat-Maḥal

In Lal-Kuan Bazar, west of Hauz-Qazi lies a large enclosure with arched pavilions and an imposing gateway with oriel windows on the road. Known as Zīnat-Maḥal, it was built in 1846 by Zīnat-Maḥal, favourite wife of Bahādur Shāh II (1837-57). A verse composed by the king and containing his *nom de plume* Ẓafar is inscribed on the arch of the gateway.

E. Fatehpuri-Masjid

At the western end of Chandni-Chowk stands the large Fatehpuri-masjid of red sandstone, with single and double-storeyed apartments on the sides and the prayer-hall at the western end broken by seven arched openings, the central one being the highest. It is surmounted by a single dome and flanked by tall minarets. It was built in 1650 by Fateḥpurī-Begam, one of the wives of Shāh Jahān.

F. Ghālib's house

A house, where the famous Urdu poet Mīrzā Ghālib (1796-1869) is said to have lived for a long time in Delhi, is situated near the corner of Ballimaran (approached from Chandni-Chowk) and Gali-Qasim-Jan. Originally the house consisted of arched corridors on three sides enclosing an open courtyard. It has been since considerably renovated and is used now for shops. Mīrzā Ghālib's grave lies in Nizamuddin (p. 117).

G. Gurudwara-Sīsganj

Gurudwara-Sīsganj near the police-station (Kotwali) in Chandni-Chowk, although built later and extended from time to time, commemorates the site where the ninth *guru* of the Sikhs, Guru Tegh Bahādur, was beheaded in 1675 by the order of emperor Aurangzeb.

H. Begam Samru's palace

Approached from Chandni-Chowk by a road between the Kumar Talkies and the State Bank of India is a large building with massive columns, now known as Bhagirath Palace, which was the palace of Begam Samru, a Muslim girl born in 1753, who embraced Christianity and married Walter Reinhard, otherwise known as Sombre (from which Samru is derived), a mercenary soldier and holder of the fief of Sardhana in Meerut District. The Begam held the fief after Reinhard's death and died in 1836 after an eventful political life.

I. Magazine gateways

In front of the General Post Office south of Kashmiri Gate stand two gateways, which mark the site of the old magazine blown up in 1857 during the Mutiny.

J. Jāmi'-Masjid

Lying about 500 m west of the Red Fort, the Jāmi'-Masjid (pl. XVIII B), the largest mosque in India, was begun by Shāh Jahān in 1650 and completed after six years at a cost of about ten lakhs of rupees. Standing on a rock and rising from a high platform provided with flights of steps on the east, north and south, its courtyard is approached through double-storeyed gateways, the main entrance being on the east. The courtyard measures nearly 100 m sq. and is enclosed by pillared corridors with domed pavilions at the corners. The rectangular prayer-hall on the west, 61 m by 27·5 m, has a magnificent facade of eleven arches, the central one being higher. It is two-bay in depth, the western bay pierced by only seven arches. The arches are decorated with marble frames, while above them run inscriptional panels in black and white marble. The prayer-hall is surmounted by three shapely domes ornamented with alternating stripes of black and white marble and is flanked at the eastern corners by tall four-storeyed tapering minarets.

The mosque has undergone considerable repairs. It was used both by the emperor and his subjects, the upper storey over the eastern gateway being intended largely for the royalty.

K. Sunahrī-Masjid

Outside the Delhi Gate of the Red Fort and opposite the Netaji Subhash Park (old Edward Park) on the new road connecting the Subhash Road with the Mahatma Gandhi Road (National Highway) stands the Sunahrī-Masjid, surmounted by its three domes, originally gilt with copper, and flanked by two minarets. Its central arch bears an inscription from which we learn that it was built in 1751 by Nawab Quḍsiya Begam, wife of Aḥmad Shāh (1748-54). It was repaired in 1852 by Bahādur Shāh II, who replaced the copper plates of the damaged domes by sandstone facing.

L. Zīnatu'l-Masājid

The Zīnatu'l-Masājid or Ghata-Masjid lying along the walls of Shāhjahānābād in Daryaganj consists of a spacious courtyard raised on a platform of basement chambers, open on the north and south, with the main entrance from the latter. Its prayer-hall, faced by seven arches, is crowned by three domes and flanked by tall minarets. Like the Jāmi'-Masjid of Shāh Jahān described above, it is largely built with sandstone, and its domes are faced with alternating stripes of black and white marble. With its tall minarets, striped domes and red colour, it gives the impression of being a copy of the Jāmi'-Masjid on a smaller scale.

57. SALĪMGAṚH

Salīmgaṛh, with its thick rubble-built ramparts and circular bastions, which have undergone considerable repairs, is roughly triangular on plan and stands to the north-east of the Red Fort on the bank of the Yamuna. It is believed to have been built by Islām Shāh Sūr (1545-54), also known as Salīm Shāh, son and successor of Sher Shāh Sūr.

58. LAL-QILA OR RED FORT

A. Ramparts and gateways

After transferring his capital to Delhi from Agra in 1638 Shāh Jahān commenced the construction of Shāhjahānābād (p. 142), and a little later, on the 16th April, 1639, he also laid the foundation of his citadel, Lal-Qila (Lāl-Qal'a) or Red Fort, known also by other names in contemporary accounts. It was completed after nine years on the 16th April 1648. The entire fort is said to have cost about one crore of rupees, half of it on the palaces.

The Red Fort, so called because of the red colour of the stone largely used in it, is octagonal on plan, with two longer sides on the east and west. On the north the fort is connected by a bridge with Salīmgaṛh. It measures about 900 m by 550 m, with its rampart walls covering a perimeter of 2·41 km and rising to a height of 33·5 m on the town side and 18 m along the river. Outside the ramparts runs a moat, originally connected with the river.

The palaces lie along the eastern side of the fort, while two imposing three-storeyed main gateways flanked by semi-octagonal towers and consisting of several apartments are located in the centre of the western and southern sides and are known as the Lahori and Delhi Gates respectively (pl. XXII). On the outside, the Delhi gate is flanked by the statues of two elephants renewed in 1903 by Lord Curzon in place of the ones which had been demolished long ago by Aurangzeb. The main entrance to the fort lies through the Lahori Gate and the palaces are reached through a roofed passage, flanked by arcaded apartments called Chhatta-Chowk and now used as shops. The other portions were originally occupied by the residences of the courtiers and the retinue. Both the gates were provided later by barbicans by Aurangzeb. There exist three other entrances on other sides, now largely closed.

The master-builders of the Red Fort were Hamīd

and Aḥmad while the construction was supervised by other officers, who were amply rewarded by the emperor by appointing them to high positions.

Most of the buildings in the fort were once occupied by the British army and bear scars of vandalistic acts inflicted on them. Quite a number of the structures were in bad state and were removed after the Mutiny.

B. Naubat-or Naqqār-Khāna

The Naubat- or Naqqār-Khāna ('drum house') stands at the entrance of the palace area, and was used for playing music five times a day at propitious hours. It was also called Hāthīpol, as visitors dismounted from their elephants (*hāthī*) here. Faced with red stone, it is a large three-storeyed building, rectangular on plan. Carved designs on its red stone walls appear to have been originally painted with gold, while the interior was painted in other colours. Several layers of these paintings can be traced even now in the entrance-chamber.

The later Mughal kings Jahāndār Shāh (1712-13) and Farrukhsiyar (1713-19) are said to have been murdered in the Naubat-Khāna. The War Memorial Museum is now housed in its upper storey.

C. Dīwān-i-'Ām

The Dīwān-i-'Ām ('hall of public audience') is the next building reached by the visitor. Originally it had a courtyard on its front. The hall proper, three bays in depth, originally ornamented with gilded stucco work and hung with heavy curtains, is raised on arches springing from pillars and has an impressive façade of nine openings of engrailed arches. At its back stands a marble canopy or baldachin, covered by its 'Bengal' roof, under which stood the emperor's throne (pl.XXIII). The emperor received the general public here and heard their complaints. A marble dais, inlaid with precious stones, stands below the throne and was used by the prime minister for receiving the complaints and petitions.

At the back of the canopy the wall is faced with beautiful panels inlaid with multicoloured stones, representing flowers and birds. These panels are said to have been executed by Austin de Bordeaux, Florentine jeweller. In the central panel on the top is shown the Greek god Orpheus with his lute. The panels were much damaged and at one time removed to the Victoria and Albert Museum in London, but were restored in 1903 at the instance of Lord Curzon.

D. Mumtāz Maḥal

There existed originally six main palaces along the river front, with the Nahr-i-Bihis͟ht ('stream of paradise') flowing through them. One of these to the north of the Mumtāz-Maḥal, called Chhoṭī Baiṭhak, has disappeared. The Mumtāz-Mahal is at the southern end of the extant row of palaces. Built with marble in its lower half of walls and pillars, it consists of six apartments divided by arched piers, and originally painted on the interior.

It formed part of the imperial seraglio. The Delhi Museum of Archaeology, consisting largely of exhibits of the Mughal period, is now housed inside it.

E. Rang-Maḥal

The Rang-Maḥal, resting on a basement, consists of a large hall, originally painted on the interior, from which it derives its name, meaning the 'palace of colour'. Divided into six apartments by engrailed arches set on piers, the two apartments on its northern and southern ends contain marble dados. Over the walls and ceilings of these apartments are embedded tiny pieces of mirror, which reflect a burning match or other light and create thus a picturesque effect. These apartments are known as Shīsh-Maḥal ('house of mirrors').

The building was part of the imperial seraglio. Through its centre along its length flowed the channel known as Nahr-i-Bihisht. In its centre is a marble basin, which is said to have been provided originally with an ivory fountain.

F. Khāṣ-Maḥal

The Khāṣ-Maḥal ('private palace') consists of three parts. The set of three rooms facing the Dīwān-i-Khās is called Tasbīḥ-Khāna ('chamber for telling beads') and was used for private worship by the emperor. The three rooms behind it are known as Khwābgāh ('sleeping chamber'). To its south a long hall with its painted walls and ceiling and a perforated screen on the west is known either as Tosh-Khāna ('robe chamber') or Baiṭhak ('sitting room'). There exists a beautiful marble screen at the northern end of these rooms carved with a 'Scale of Justice' suspended over a crescent surrounded with stars and clouds (pl. XXIV).

Below this and other palaces were organised animal-fights, such as between lions and elephants, which could be viewed by the emperor and royal ladies from these palaces.

There is an inscription over the southern arch of the Khwābgāh, from which we learn that the building was begun in 1048 A.H. (1639) and completed in 1058 A.H. (1648) at a cost of fifty lakhs of rupees, which probably refers to the expenditure incurred on all the palaces.

G. Muthamman-Burj

Adjoining the eastern wall of the Khwābgāh is a semi-octagonal tower, called Muthamman-Burj ('octagonal tower'), where the emperor appeared every morning before his subjects, the ceremony being known as *darshan*. A balcony projecting from the central side of the Muthamman-Burj was constructed in 1223 A.H. (1808-09) by Akbar II (1806-37), as stated by him in an inscription over its arches. It was from this balcony that King George V and Queen Mary appeared before the public in 1911.

H. Dīwān-i-Khāṣ

The Dīwān-i-Khāṣ ('hall of private audience') with openings of engrailed arches on its sides consists of a rectangular central chamber surrounded by aisles of arches rising from piers (pl. II). The lower parts of the piers are inlaid with floral designs, while the upper portions are gilded and painted. The present wooden ceiling of the hall was painted in 1911. The four corners of its roof are surmounted by pillared *chhatrīs*.

Over the marble pedestal in its centre stood the famous Peacock Throne which was removed in 1739 by Nādir Shāh. Through the centre of the hall flowed the Nahr-i-Bihisht. Over the corner-arches of the northern and southern walls below the cornice is inscribed the famous verse of Amīr Khusraw exclaiming 'If there be a paradise on the earth, it is this, it is this, it is this'.

The hall was used by the emperor for giving private audience to the selected courtiers and visitors. Originally there existed on the west of the Dīwān-i-Khāṣ two enclosures, one for the nobles and the other for those who were not of a very high rank. These enclosures were removed after the Mutiny. During the Mutiny Bahādur Shāh II held court in the Dīwān-i-Khāṣ.

I. Ḥammām

On the north of the Dīwān-i-Khās lies the bath-room set or Ḥammām, consisting of three apartments separated by corridors. The floors and dados of these apartments are built with marble, inlaid with floral patterns of multicoloured stones. The two rooms on either side of the present entrance were used, it is believed, by the royal children for their bath. The eastern apartment, with three fountain basins, one of which is reputed to have emitted rose-water, was used mainly as the dressing room. There is a basin in the middle of the central room. The western apartment was used for hot or vapour bath, the heating arrangement being fixed in its western wall.

J. Motī-Masjid

To the west of the Ḥammām lies the small mosque, called the Motī-Masjid ('pearl mosque'), built by Aurangzeb for his personal use. The prayer-hall of the mosque is inlaid with outlines of *musallās* (small carpets for prayers) in black marble, and it stands at a higher level than the courtyard. The hall is surmounted by three bulbous domes, originally copper-plated, which appear to be too constricted at the neck (pl. II). The eastern door is provided with copper-plated leaves. The mosque was also used by the ladies of the seraglio.

K. Ḥayāt-Bakhsh garden and pavilions

The area north of the Motī-Masjid is occupied by a garden, called the Ḥayāt-Bakhsh-Bāgh ('life-bestowing garden'), divided into squares on the pattern of Mughal gardens with causeways and channels between them. It finds mention in the contemporary accounts, although its present layout is new.

At the north-eastern corner of the garden is a tower, called Shāh-Burj, now domeless, which suffered much during the Mutiny. A similar tower known as

Asad-Burj stands on the south-eastern corner of the fort. The water for feeding the Nahr-i-Bihisht was apparently lifted up to the Shāh-Burj from the river and then carried by channels to the various palaces. The present pavilion adjoining the tower on the south was perhaps built during Aurangzeb's reign. In the centre of the north wall is a marble cascade sloping into a 'scalloped' basin.

Two other marble pavilions in the centre of the northern and southern sides of the garden are known as Sāwan and Bhādon, two principal months of the rainy season, either because they represent those months or were used during those months, but which is Sāwan and which is Bhādon is not exactly certain. The northern one is provided with a tank with niches for candles in its sides, so that the water cascading over them would create a picturesque effect.

On the elevated strip of land along the eastern wall stood two small marble pavilions, built by Bahādur Shāh II, the northern one known as Motī-Mahal and the southern one as Hīra-Mahal. The former was removed after the Mutiny; the latter still stands. In the centre of the garden is a large tank with a red stone pavilion in its middle, originally connected by a causeway with the garden. It is known as Zafar-Mahal, after the *nom de plume* of Bahādur Shāh II, by whom it was built, in about 1842.

SELECT BIBLIOGRAPHY

Bashīru'd-Dīn Aḥmad, *Wāqi'āt-i-Dāru'l-Ḥukūmāt-i-Dihlī*, 3 vols. (Agra, 1919).

Percy Brown, *Indian Architecture* (Islamic Period), 5th Ed., (Bombay, 1968).

Alexander Cunningham, *Archaeological Survey of India Reports*, Vol. I (Simla, 1871), pp. 132-231; Vol. IV (Calcutta, 1874), pp. 1-91; Vol. XX (Calcutta, 1885), pp. 142-161.

H.C. Fanshawe, *Delhi Past and Present* (London, 1902).

G.R. Hearn, *The Seven Cities of Delhi* (London 1906).

H.G. Keene, *Handbook for visitors to Delhi*, rewritten by E.A. Duncan (Calcutta, 1906).

Sayyid Aḥmad Khān, *Āthār-us-Sanādīd* (Delhi, 1847, and Cawnpore, 1904).

H. Sharp, *Delhi: its Story and Buildings* (Delhi, 1921).

T.G.P. Spear, *Delhi: A Historical Sketch* (Bombay, 1945).

Carr Stephen, *The Archaeology and Monumental Remains of Delhi*, (Ludhiana and Calcutta, 1876).

Tatsuro Yamamoto, Matsuo Ara and Tokifusa Tsukinowa, *Delhi: Architectural Remains of the Delhi Sultanate Period*, 3 vols., (Tokyo, 1968-70).

INDEX TO MONUMENTS[1]

[1]This index only includes monuments in Delhi. The references where a monument is described in some detail are printed in italics.